BEYOND XAVIERA

To Acapulco . . . for sultry days around the pool, and even hotter nights with Francine, Penny, and Lizbeth.

To Nassau . . . where Vanessa introduces Larry to a whole new trip around the bathroom, bedroom, and balcony.

To Las Vegas . . . for a high rolling weekend and an unpredictable, unforgettable Oriental chick.

To Los Angeles . . . where Larry meets Jane, the swinging Amazon doll . . . and plays Tarzan.

To Toronto . . . with Cathy, who knew mor~ about massage than most men coul~

To New York . . . ~~
ful Vanessa, above~

Beyond Xaviera

by Larry
"The Silver Fox"

PINNACLE BOOKS • NEW YORK CITY

BEYOND XAVIERA! . . .

An original Pinnacle Books edition,
published for the first time anywhere.

ISBN: 0-523-00707-8

First printing, August 1975

Printed in the United States of America

PINNACLE BOOKS, INC.
275 Madison Avenue
New York, N. Y. 10016

To the lovely and wonderful
Pauline Rivelli,
Without whom this book
could never have been . . .

BEYOND XAVIERA

CONTENTS

Introduction

One Plus One Equals One

There is an epitaph that reads:

*Once I wasn't,
Then I was,
And now I ain't again ...*

This statement sums up my three-year associa-tion with Xaviera Hollander, the Happy Hooker. I've already written a lot about her and me in my previous book, *My Life With Xaviera, "The Happy Hooker,"* but now there's a different story to tell.

An epitaph appears on a tombstone, let's say this one applies to a part of my life that's dead— all in the past, but I am far from dead now! In fact, I was reborn when I met Vanessa, who is

1

more to me than the Happy Hooker ever was, and she's what this book is all about.

Vanessa is better than the Happy Hooker in *and* out of bed. She is a great sex partner. She has dignity, and she's mine and mine alone. Therein lies the supreme difference between Xaviera and Vanessa. Vanessa's my own private whore, and let's just say Xaviera was less discriminating or discreet.

Vanessa and I both feel we have something special, so we both tell our stories here.

Although two people are talking to you, we are, in essence, one. Few people experience the ultimate in a relationship, and it is our sincere wish that you, dear reader, find the happiness Vanessa and I share as "one."

If you have read all of Xaviera's books, as well as mine, *My Life With Xaviera,* you may have noticed that very little mention—if any at all—was made of genuine love, tenderness, compassion, warmth, or caring. This is how it was with Xaviera and me. Her life was sex-sex-sex—with me, with others, heterosexual relationships, homosexual relationships, in groups, shows, and swings that would startle the most sexually liberated.

Now, I'm not putting sex down, but after these escapades, I'd gladly revert to my former "old-fashioned" way of thinking. There's nothing like having a woman who is totally your own. A woman whose heart and whose cunt are totally

2

yours. *One* cunt for *one* "visitor," instead of a cunt that's been visited by so many strange cocks that you're just one of a million sexual exploits.

Every man should have his own personal whore. A lady whore. Talk to a few men, or women for that matter, and you'll see it's not as strange as it sounds. Every woman wants to be a whore to her man, and every man wants to be his whore's only man. The desire to give and receive ultimate pleasure is all it takes. Whether one knows a variety of sexual gymnastics or not, when two people give *all* of themselves to each other, that's giving to the fullest.

Active spiritually, intellectually, socially, emotionally, and sexually, Vanessa, my lady whore, gives herself totally in and out of bed. She performs all the sexual acts needed to please me, and I do my best to keep her active cunt happy. We don't fuck because we feel we have to. We want to spend long hours languishing in bed, slowly exploring each other's bodies and passions. I know that as far as she's concerned, I fulfill her needs and she's not looking for a substitute right now.

My lady is many things . . .

Her socks get mixed up with mine in the laundry. A casual dresser at times, she prefers calf-length socks with pants, and "old-fashioned" garter belt and stockings when dressing up. (A real "turn-on" when she's *undressing*.) She'd wear panty hose, but insists they're inconvenient.

3

They'd be awkward if we felt like fucking in the car!

She likes old late-night TV movies as much as I do; the sort of soppy, sentimental ones where boy wins girl. Sometimes she looks like my kid brother; yet she can look as feminine, glamorous, and sexy as any movie star.

She loves to play house. She loves to talk ... to tell me about her day and how much she digs the times we're together.

(Here's what Vanessa's got to say. Whenever you see italic type it is Vanessa speaking. She's not italic, she just talks that way.)

Oh, Larry makes me sound like such a sweet little girlfriend, but he didn't mention that I'm the one who loves to fuck him—to suck him until my entire face is wet—to eat every part of him. When we're relaxing together, I'll sneak over and gently suck his beautiful cock, kiss it, pass my wet lips over the tip of his cock and put my tongue deep into it, and wipe his wet prick by running it gently through my hair. Not an inch of him escapes my hungry lips and roving tongue. I suck his big toe with the same delicacy I give his cock.

When Larry comes in my mouth, I take him in fully and swallow that part of him which flows from him to me. This, to me, is a complete bond of love. I have never fucked and sucked anyone so

4

completely before. But, then, what I feel with Larry, I have never felt with anyone else. Larry's fluid, a part of his inner being, flowing inside me, joining my blood and becoming part of my body, is total union. We become one.

I'm the one who puts her sensuous nipples in his ass—wetting him first with my tongue—and fucks him in the ass, one nipple at a time.

I'm the one who loves to rub her wet, hot cunt on his chest, then down to his stomach, and ultimately finds his big, hard cock waiting for my pulsating, aching cunt. A beautiful prick that always finds its way to my cunt as if a magnet were drawing my cunt and Larry's cock together where they belong.

Each time we fuck, there's the novelty and sensation of our first time together—deep penetration, just a little twinge of sweet pain, and then Larry's cock bursting inside me like a rocket.

No matter what our method of foreplay, whether it be in bed, in the tub, the shower, rubbing his cock between my legs while standing up, eating each other, fucking me from behind, or me astride him—the great old-fashioned he-on-me fucking is the ultimate. I have no unfulfilled fantasies because Larry satisfies all of my desires.

I like "private" love—just two people—no sadomasochism and no one watching. I know Larry's life was different before we met. Orgies, partousses, and swings were a big part of his days with Xaviera. He may miss some of these

5

turn-ons, and should he decide he misses them too much to keep away from them, he is free to go back to the jungle. I want to fulfill his every need alone. Larry may like his captivity. We are two free-spirited people, each knowing that we can split at any time. There are no ties, no legal bonds to hold us. Only human ones. Each other. I may stop loving him, or he may leave me, but I'll never stop loving the days and nights in which I loved him.

Beyond Xaviera, and into Vanessa

The most frequent question I am asked is, "How did you first meet Xaviera?" It follows that the same curiosity should be aroused as to how I first met Vanessa.

A long time passed from the first time I *saw* Vanessa until I actually *met* her. It wasn't terribly complicated. I had a habit of hanging out in the office of Pat, a lovely young executive, while waiting for my friend Aaron. I'd wait in her office, use the telephone, and pass the time of day until Aaron would finish his business commitments and we could escape for lunch or for a social evening. Vanessa had walked past Pat's office many times, and I had wondered who she was. As far as I could see, she was the prettiest gal on the floor. But she never stopped for even a casual hello. On a few occasions she'd look into the office while I was alone, and I wouldn't get as much as a smile as she continued down the hall. Letting my curiosity get the better of my good sense, I asked Pat who this mystery lady was, and learned nothing more than that she was Pat's boss. Pat didn't volunteer any other information. I got the same cold shoulder when I asked Aaron. I felt like the big bad wolf when he answered, "Hey, she's a good girl. Stay away."

Still wondering, but to no avail, I watched her parade around the office. About a year later Vanessa ran into Pat's office, not noticing I was there. I walked over to her to introduce myself. I shook hands with her, and then she turned around and left. Nearly a half-hour later, she returned to ask me two questions about Xaviera. I immediately rattled off the answers, and returned a question of my own—"Will you have lunch with me?"

I got an equally hurried, "No, thank you," with a final, "let me finish the book first."

A few weeks later, with my car in the repair shop, I had my friend Dan chauffeuring me about in his car. In heavy traffic, waiting for the red light to change, I was eyeballing everything that was moving on the sidewalk. As coincidence would have it, there was Vanessa. As she was about to cross the street, I called over to her half jokingly, "How about our lunch date? Did you finish the book?"

8

She quickly replied, "Sure, I finished the book. How about P.J. Clark's?"

"When?" I asked.

"About a half-hour."

The light changed, and Dan and I continued on our way.

Leaving Dan with the motor running, I ran into P.J.'s, and lo and behold, there was Vanessa with two other women, all of them attractive. Wow! Three good-looking girls for lunch.

As I walked over, Vanessa stood up and introduced me to her two companions—her sister and her friend. Taking me by the arm, she led me to another table adjoining theirs. Over lunch and some drinks, I learned the meaning of "Beauty's only skin deep." The more we talked, the more I knew this was a lady I wanted to get to know well . . . a lady I would want all for myself.

To be honest, I can't say I was intrigued by Larry before we actually met. The first time I saw the Silver Fox, he was roaming the corridors of my office. President of my own firm and a few others, before we met I was made an offer I couldn't refuse, and closed the eyelids of my own business and joined this larger company.

Larry was known as "Larry, the pimp," around the office. A title earned by his reputation among several executives in the company. When I'd pass the office of Pat, one of my associates, I'd often spot Larry on the phone or discussing the business aspects of Xaviera's books, since he was Xaviera's business manager.

"So, that's a pimp!" I'd think to myself, catching myself to avoid gawking.

Pat kept Larry to herself. Though curious at times, I really didn't care since, I certainly wasn't interested in meeting a pimp. When he would leave, all I heard from Pat was "Larry this and Larry that." She would crow about Larry the pimp, his escapades, and stress the fact that Larry had a missing finger. Her fascination at this was beyond me, but at one point unable to bear her constant prattle, I glibly responded, "He probably left it up some hooker's ass!"

Since I kept seeing Larry around the office and people kept talking about him, I decided to read Xaviera. I read chapters while on the toilet, or at bedtime, or before a date.

Having recently been divorced and vowing never to marry again, I was having a great time dating many marvelous men. I was calling my own shots, and I liked my new freedom. Until I was legally divorced, I avoided affairs outside my marriage. I felt it was my wifely duty to be faithful. But now, free from the constraints of marriage and a strict Catholic upbringing, I had several satisfying lovers and occasional casual affairs. As I read Xaviera, I kept waiting for two questions to be answered. First, what was Xaviera's birth control method? and, second, what was her astrological sign?

About three quarters through the book I was introduced to Larry. One high-pressured day at the office, I blindly whizzed into Pat's office to discuss a project on which we were collaborating. I burst into her office in my usual fast, direct manner, and there was Larry.

"Oh, er, ah, have you ever met Larry Drey﹨ fuss?" she flustered, knowing damn well I never had and sounding like she wished I hadn't barged in so unexpectedly.

"No," I said, in my confident, buoyant way. I shook his hand, looked him in the eyes, and rattled, "By the way, I'm reading Xaviera! Returning my gaze, he replied, "Great! How do you like it?" "I find her pretty honest," I answered, "but how can she live at that pace! She literally fucked everything that moved! By the way, I have two questions that haven't been answered yet."

Larry answered them in his fast, rapid-fire speech. Her birth control device was a diaphragm coated with Koromex jelly, and her sun sign was Gemini.

As I was leaving the office, I turned in the doorway and told Pat, "I'll come back when you're free." Larry kept looking at me. I could tell he was anxious to talk some more.

"Have you finished the book yet?"

"No," I said, "I have a few more chapters to go."

"Let me know when you finish it. I'll buy you lunch," Larry smiled.

"Great!" I smiled back, not wanting to sound impolite. In my mind I thought, "Fuck you, mister, who needs a pimp—to buy me lunch?"

I didn't find Larry attractive at first. In fact, having been in the music business for several years, Larry reminded me of the aging record company executive who tries to look hip to conform with the young rock stars who record for the label.

Larry had long but beautifully silvered hair, and wore gold chains around his neck, and an open-necked, gaudily patterned shirt that fell over his belly like a ruffled curtain.

Exit pimp.

As fate would have it, I met Larry again purely by accident. Jauntily returning to my office building one sunny day in early July and feeling quite pleased with myself after a successful meeting with a client, I spied Larry in a car waiting for the light to turn green. As I crossed, we waved to each other.

"How about that lunch?" Larry asked. "Have you finished the book?"

"Yes, I did," I responded with raised eyebrows. "Yes, I'll have that lunch. Meet me in P.J. Clark's at noon."

What Larry didn't know was that I was to meet my sister and her friend there for lunch at noon. Feeling safe and secure with my big sister

*and rather uninspired by Xaviera prompted me
to be cocksure of myself.*

*I never thought Larry would show, but at
12:20 he eased his way through the crowds to
our table. Before Larry's arrival I warned the
girls that I was to meet Xaviera Hollander's
pimp and asked them to hang around until he
left. "Don't leave me alone with this character," I
pleaded. "I really put my foot in it by inviting
him here."*

*To my alarm, dear sister, who is always ready
for the unexpected, found it terribly exciting, and
my hopes of a united front drooped.*

*Introductions were made, and Larry and I sat
at the adjoining table, and he ordered our drinks.
In ten minutes of staccato speech, Larry rattled
off the names of all the important people he knew
and flew into a discourse faster than a bullet
meets its mark. I wasn't impressed with the
names he mentioned. I was more amazed by his
incessant talking and flitting from topic to topic.
I asked him his sun sign. Larry is a Gemini, and
it all seemed to make sense; well, astrologically
at least.*

*Before I could catch my breath, he was off on
something else. "I'm going away for the 4th and
into the weekend," Larry said. "May I call you
when I get back? What's your phone number?"*

*"Call me at my office," I said, still not sure this
was a man I wanted as a friend.*

Larry didn't stay for lunch. Instead, he paid

for the drinks at our table and at my sister's as well and then rushed out to his waiting car and chauffeur. A nice gesture, I thought, a man from the old school who believes ladies shouldn't pay for their own drinks.

(Larry speaks.)

After my days with Xaviera, I found it a pleasant break to meet a lady I could talk to. I never said much to Xaviera when we were alone that didn't pertain to one thing ... You guessed it—SEX!

Don't get me wrong, Vanessa is a real good looker, but there was something way beyond my first physical attraction that was drawing me toward her. Even in our conversations I could sense that Vanessa was a giving person, a person who would gladly give all of herself to the right man. Something was telling me I wanted to try being "the right man" for Vanessa.

When I think of how intimate our relationship has become, how well I know her body and what turns her on, like my tongue circling her sensuous nipples, I could laugh out loud as I think of our first date.

The first time out with her, and we were both thoroughly drunk. Vanessa vetoes my suggestion of dinner at a quiet bistro, and offers to cook dinner at her home. Back at her apartment, my eyes exploring her glorious body, I thought of all the delights to be found in her arms, and then thought the better of the whole idea and sat down to a TV movie while she cooked dinner. At midnight, the perfect gentleman, I left. There was something about Vanessa, something disarming and beautiful, that made me want to make her much more than one pleasurable experience.

Wednesday, the Fourth of July, came and went. Thursday I was back at my desk, and, surprisingly, Larry called.

"Mr. Dreyfuss on the phone" my secretary announced. It seems Larry didn't go away for the weekend, and would I have dinner with him on Friday?

Now Fridays were usually booked for me, but here again fate was playing its game, and I didn't have anything planned for that particular Friday evening. As a matter of fact I hadn't made definite plans for any night that weekend because the weather had been so inconsistent.

I arrived at my apartment about 4:30. No sooner did I get in than the phone rang. (I had given him my unlisted home phone number by this time.) It was Larry. He had a 5:30 appointment with his hair stylist, Mr. Sal, located in the Hilton Hotel. Since it was in the neighborhood, I asked him to come over and kill some time before his appointment.

He accepted. The date was July 6, 1973.

To say I was curious about Larry is an under-

15

statement. What did the "Silver Fox" have that made Xaviera choose him as her steady boyfriend? Good in the hay was my first thought. If he wasn't good at the beginning of their courtship, she must have taught him some neat tricks. Maybe I could learn something from this cat, but my first thoughts weren't sexual. I was intrigued by the mystique surrounding a nice, middle-aged, respectable man who got mixed up with a hooker. How does a guy go for a woman who's fucked and sucked dozens of men and women all week and returns to him on weekends?

I made one promise to myself I would not go to bed with this man. No matter how curious I was, or how certain he might be that the evening would end in bed, I wasn't going to be just another conquest.

July 6, 1973—No Sex

Larry arrived at my apartment about ten minutes after he phoned. I had opened a bottle of champagne and was feeling quite bubbly by the time he got there. I looked quite well too, wearing a clingy, bright orange halter dress that showed my small, but sensuous breasts, and fell to my form, revealing that I wore nothing underneath. A good tan, a vibrant orange dress, and bare feet. I greeted Larry at the door with a glass of chilled champagne. He looked surprised, yet pleased.

"Nice place," said Larry as he looked around my small, but stylish apartment.

"This is it," I said. "Small, but it's my own."

We sat on the couch and talked about nothing in particular. Larry admired some things I had in the apartment, and I explained where they came from—Europe, wherever—and that most of the things were salvaged from my three-year marriage.

It was soon time for Larry to leave for his hairdressing appointment. True to the compulsive Gemini character, Larry changed our plans and decided I was to go along with him.

"He's Italian too, like you. I'm sure you'll enjoy him."

"Wait for me just one minute. I'll get out of this dress and change into something less dramatic. Walking the streets of New York in this dress would guarantee rape," I said. "Ummm, maybe I'll keep it on!" I grinned devilishly.

Larry laughed, and I suddenly realized he was sort of attractive, especially when he smiled. Dressed and ready to go, I slyly slipped a split of champagne into my oversized purse, along with a champagne glass, and we were off.

I served Larry the champagne while Mr. Sal worked on his hair. Mr. Sal warned Larry that he would become spoiled by the attention I was paying him, and I should "watch out" or Larry would expect this treatment all the time. We all laughed, and I assured Mr. Sal in Italian that we had only just met, and we probably wouldn't see each other again. I didn't want to hurt Larry by revealing to him that curiosity alone had made me accept this date.

Larry suggested eating out, but that didn't hold as much attraction for me as it had earlier, so I suggested I cook dinner at my place. Not only do I love to cook, but I was thoroughly "champagned" and didn't feel like facing a crowded restaurant. Remembering we both dined out most of the time and needed a pleasant break, Larry agreed and positioned himself in front of the TV while I got things together in the kitchen.

After a good dinner and some quiet conversation, Larry asked me to spend Saturday with him, if I was free.

"OK," I said, explaining once again that it was a lucky coincidence that I didn't have any plans for the weekend, and made some comment about my hopes for good weather.

Larry left soon after midnight. I liked him.

July 9, 1973—(Three Days Late, But It Sure Started With a "Bang")

The strange, yet impressive aspect of our "first date" was that neither Larry or I leaped into bed right away. Oh we both had it in our heads (!), for sure, but I was sparring with Larry at first. Strange, because here was the notorious sex symbol, "the Silver Fox," the one who satisfied the insatiable Xaviera, yet I wasn't anxious to discover his talents. Impressive because Larry didn't come on—as his public expects—with the immediate "you wanna fuck?" attitude.

The chemistry was there all right. We both knew that. As I look back, I think we were both waiting for the other to make the first move— towards the bedroom, that is.

There's a difference between fucking and making love. That first time in bed with Larry was indescribable. A seductive wrestling match; each one wanting to make the first overture in lovemaking. Ordinarily I'm the aggressor, but with Larry there was no contest.

We had been out on the town that evening—a pleasant dinner, wine, and music. Then dancing at the local disco. The city was hot and muggy, and it was good to get back to my air-conditioned apartment.

I poured two snifters of brandy as I announced to Larry that I was going to take a hot bath, with bubbles.

"Let me know when you're under the bubbles, so I can come in and join you," Larry said nonchalantly.

With a silent chorus of "I'm Forever Blowin' Bubbles" and thinking what a happy broad she must be, I disappeared into the bathroom and settled in the full, hot, dreamy bubble bath. I didn't tell Larry to join me, nor did he barge into my private luxury. We were still both playing it very cool.

19

As I dried myself, Larry called, "Are you OK?"

"I'm fine," I said as I slipped into a robe.

I opened the bathroom door to find Larry stripped to his bikini undershorts.

"I'm taking a fast shower, OK?"

"Be my guest," I said as I closed the door and left. When the shower turned off, I knew Larry was finished with his chore. I opened the bathroom door and peered in.

"I'll help you dry," I said, and I caressed him with a big towel and kissed his wet lips.

(*Larry*: Not a bad beginning, no matter how you look at it. A thoroughly "clean" one, anyway.)

Love Will Lick Anything

After our Saturday together, things started happening fast. We both had a week's vacation coming up, and before we knew it, we were packed and headed for Las Vegas. I felt as though we were growing together. Things were going well with Vanessa, and then, suddenly, I thought it was all over. We had a ball in Vegas. It was on the way back ...

I had taken some of the unfinished manuscript for the book I was doing called *My Life With Xaviera*, so that I could edit some of the chapters. Innocently enough, I gave them to Vanessa to take a quick look. There was no sex in those chapters, but you'd think I'd given her a cobra. After only a few moments of reading them, she very curtly handed me my papers, and with a touch of hurt in her voice, said "Larry, I'm not for you. You need another hooker maybe, but not me. Better yet, why don't you just go to Canada, and tell Xaviera how much you really love her."

I was bewildered. What the hell was the matter now? "We just had a fantastic five days at the Flamingo Hotel in Las Vegas. What's going on?"

The conversation ceased. As we drove back to Vanessa's apartment, somewhere between my anger and bewilderment, I felt the whole thing was going to end right then and there.

... So Larry was bewildered, couldn't understand why I was angry, had no idea of how deeply I was hurt. He handed the manuscript to me on a flight back from Las Vegas where we had spent five days, five days of love, passion, and complete giving of ourselves.

What timing. I was filled with all sorts of beautiful thoughts of Larry and me. We had practically fucked every night away. He'd fuck me in my ass, my cunt, my mouth, and come all over me—in torrents at times. I loved every minute of him. I used to lick and suck his whole body; he tasted so good. Of all the men I knew there was really no one before who made me feel this great sense of love.

I didn't realize myself how much I had come to love him until he handed me the manuscript that night and asked me to read some of the chapters. "You stupid bitch!" I cursed to myself. "You had to fall for a guy who's a swinger, a pimp for some whore. When are you going to learn?"

This was a complete bursting of my bubble. A complete reversal of what I thought about Larry. So what do you do, Vanessa? Just exit from this guy! Quit. Remember it as a beautiful experience, nothing more. Walk away as you've walked away from so many other so-called romances.

What I found out later, was that the manuscript he gave me to read was written seven months before we met.

By then I had let Larry know I'd had it. I'd been deceived. I'd been hurt, and I didn't want to see him again. Larry called me the very next day and apologized for showing me the manuscript. He shouldn't have shown it to me. He asked me what I was doing that evening. I had turned down two dinner dates; I couldn't bring myself to see anyone else. I just wanted to go home and die. Larry asked if he could meet me at my place after work. Barely able to contain my happiness, I coolly replied, "5:30 or 6:00 will be fine."

We went out for dinner and drinks. We talked the night away, and eventually wound up at my apartment. As we were saying goodnight, I kissed him and coyly asked him not to leave, while I unhooked and unzipped his pants, lowered them and the silly bikini shorts that he wears, unbuttoned his shirt and threw it off his shoulders. While I nibbled on his ear, I got out of my slacks. I slipped out of my shoes and slipped out of my

23

blouse, very quickly pushing my hard nipples up against his chest as I rubbed my cunt against his beautiful cock. "Let's go to bed," I said, and we did.

Lying beside Larry in bed, I started with his earlobes, his neck, his nipples, his stomach, his navel, his thighs, his beautiful cock, his beautiful balls. I took them in my mouth. I wet my hand and tried to manipulate him so he'd come. He sucked me, he kissed me. I sucked him, I kissed him. He mounted me and fucked me until I thought I would die. He came with me and our juices intermingled. Licking him clean I said, "Larry, please don't leave tonight." And he replied very romantically, "My car is in a meter zone."

That's Larry.

Always Leave the Meter Running

My relationship with Vanessa was still in its infancy. We knew each other for only about two weeks, yet it seemed so much longer. We'd established an intimacy people seldom share. I was as happy as a man could be until ... All of a sudden problems. A long distance call from Canada shook me right out of my euphoria.

"Larry, will you please come to Toronto. Paul has a bunch of papers that need my signature." As Xaviera's agent for her new book, I called her lawyer, who had completed contracts for her signature. He wouldn't hear of my not delivering them in person.

"If you mail them, all of Canada will know what's in those contracts. Go up and get them signed and bring them back."

I hated going up because I didn't want to leave Vanessa. I didn't want to see Xaviera. And after we finished our work, there'd be other business to take care of. I didn't want any part of this selfish broad, but I knew aggravating her would be a bad idea. I couldn't carry a pacifier in my pocket. She would want the pacifier between my pockets. Oh well, business before pleasure.

Packing to leave, I figured I better try my damnedest to keep Xaviera happy while I was there. A little shopping around, and I'd collected everything she might ask for. Tubes of Koremex Jelly, the pictures left hanging on her wall, and my cock. Knowing Xaviera, that was most necessary.

Boarding the plane at Kennedy airport, I wondered just how many times I would jump at Xaviera's beck and call. Just when I think she's part of my past, she comes creeping back into my life. I had something good going for me now, and there was no way Xaviera was going to destroy it.

It didn't take too long for us to pack away the work—about ten minutes. How long could it take to sign your name a few times. Then out to the store to do some shopping. Window-shopping, the conversation was pleasant and light. I was almost glad I'd come. We stopped at the Dutch store to get the licorice I like, and filled up some cartons with food for her "fridge."

We were back home by 4 o'clock. By 4:10 I'd

changed my mind about being glad to see her. In her usual bragging manner, she'd told me about two girls coming that evening from Scranton. Two lesbians, who were anxious to see her, had sent gifts and flowers. Quite pleased with the attention she was getting from them, she didn't want to offend them by my presence. Turning on the charm, Xaviera tried to make it seem alright that I'd just flown up from New York and was unwanted.

"Larry, instead of sleeping here tonight, you take another room. I'll join you at your room after I give the girls a party. You know that I can never really get off with girls. I'll eat them, and we'll horse around, but then I'll come to your room and you can take care of me."

I saw an easy way out. "Xaviera, forget me. It's not fair to leave the girls. They came all the way from Scranton. You can't just kick them out, and you can't desert them in your apartment. Forget about me. I'll go back to New York."

She had to agree I was right. All of a sudden her face lit up. "You bastard!" Without a second glance, off came her clothes and into the bath she went. Ten minutes later she grabbed my hand and escorted me to the tub.

Soaping my back and moving down to my thighs, she slowly started fondling my balls. I knew the fight was over when her nimble fingers began manipulating the soap around my cock.

Toweling dry, we moved to the bed. Xaviera

took my prick in her mouth and was sucking hard. Shifting position, her throbbing cunt was over my face and my inquisitive tongue was exploring. As always in our favorite 69 position, we both came at the same time.

Before I'd had a chance to catch my breath, Xaviera jumped up from the bed, with a smile on her face.

"Still going to keep your date tonight? Think you'll want to fuck, or will you think of me and remember?"

Instantly I realized the reason for her big performance was to prevent my having intercourse later that night. She hoped I'd be too satisfied to even think of another woman. But I knew differently. Smiling inside and taking the necessary papers with me, I packed my bag and returned to New York City.

Over dinner that night I told Vanessa the whole story. I saw the hurt look on her face, yet I felt I did better for having told her. Realizing that what I did mattered to her, I saw how much I cared for Vanessa. I promised myself that this would never happen again. No matter how many tricks Xaviera played.

I stayed away from Xaviera for over two months. Each time she asked me why I wasn't coming up that weekend, I gave her some excuse and told her I could accomplish whatever had to be done on the telephone. I reminded her our relationship was strictly business, so if it was important enough for her to want me up there, she could reimburse me for the $100 airfare. Knowing Xaviera, I knew I'd never be invited again.

Eventually the time did come when the completed contracts were ready and had to be sent to her Swiss management company. When I called Xaviera to tell her I would be coming, she couldn't understand why I wouldn't spend the weekend at her place, since her boyfriend, Paul would be away. Refreshing her memory, I told her I was going with another girl, and was very happy and didn't want to get involved with her again. I thought I had convinced her, so up to Canada I ran.

We went over the contracts in short order. An hour's flight, for ten minutes' work, ridiculous. I was about to pack up the papers and leave the city, when all of a sudden a naked Xaviera comes parading out of the bedroom. In a second she was all over me and started taking my clothes off. I didn't want to antagonize her. I needed her until my book was published. I knew Xaviera—one false move and the whole deal would be down the drain.

With all my clothes off, she was on her knees starting to lick me all over my body. I followed her into the bedroom where we got into our favorite 69 position.

Xaviera shifted into high gear, and soon she was coming, and I held back as long as I could. She froze, then quickly turned me around so that my prick slid into her cunt. After about ten minutes she had built herself up to the point of a second orgasm, and her familiar, "Give it to me, give it to me," grew louder in my ears. I finally collapsed in her sweaty arms and lay there for about five minutes. Then she jumped up and went to the bathroom. Coming out a few minutes later looking like the cat that swallowed the canary, she said, "Larry, now tell the truth. Wasn't that the greatest? Is your new girlfriend anything like I am? Tell me the truth, ain't I still the best?"

Looking her straight in the eye, I replied, "Sure, Xaviera, you know you're the greatest in bed." Then she let me know just how great she really was, and said that any time she wanted me, I'd pick right up and come, leaving any other woman behind.

I finished packing my papers, put them in the attaché case, and walked out the front door. Little did she know the joke was on her. Larry never came that afternoon. It was all a fake.

That night I was horny as hell. Vanessa met me at LaGuardia Airport, and we had dinner at the terminal restaurant. We had just sat down when she asked, "Well, did you get another blow job?"

I smiled and told her exactly what had happened. I didn't want to lie. I told her that not only had she not given me a blow job, but that Xaviera had had a dry run that afternoon. I finished by telling her I'd missed her. A little crinkle of a smile came across her face, and she said,

"Larry, let's finish dinner as quickly as possible, and then go home. I have an idea I'd like to try."

About an hour later, we made our way to my car and arrived at Vanessa's a half-hour later.

She told me to make myself comfortable in the living room and then disappeared. I could hear the shower running. A few minutes later, clad in a bathrobe, she asked me if I wanted to shower also. On a hot summer's eve, how could anyone refuse?

Finishing my shower, I walked into the living room to be surprised by Vanessa lying naked on a fur rug in front of the lit fireplace. Behind her body I could see the flames leaping. It took me a few seconds to realize that she'd closed all the windows, turned on all the air conditioners and started the fire. Dropping my towel, I entered her eager arms. I must say I never felt the heat of the fireplace, only the heat of Vanessa's body. This had to be one of the most beautiful sexual moments of my life. I was in the arms of a woman who loved me, a woman whose cunt ached to have my prick inside, to be joined together as one.

The flames danced and crackled, the room glowed, and it was mid-July. It wasn't that I was crazy, and I was anything but cold with Larry lying next to me. One thought built my fire in mid-July—I couldn't help believing that this

31

thing with Larry was too good to be true, and it couldn't possibly last into the winter. I just had to make love with Larry in front of a roaring fire.

Air conditioners on high, champagne in our glasses, pillows and a goatskin rug our floor bed, Larry and I ... and Larry and I ... kissing, caressing, fondling, touching, hugging, and all the beautiful things that two people share.

Larry quietly took the pillow from under my head and put it under my ass, moving to my lips, to my ears, to my neck, to my shoulders, to my nipples. He kissed and sucked, and I was ready to die. And he moved down and down until he got to my cunt and sucked and kissed and tongued until I really couldn't take it any more. "Larry, I don't want to come without you."

Then Larry put his big beautiful cock in my cunt, and I said, "Fuck me, Larry, oh, Larry. Come inside me. Come with me." And he did. We lay quietly in each other's arms, and all we heard was the crackle of the logs. As the fire dimmed, we fell asleep.

I don't know how long we slept, but when we got up, it was freezing. The air conditioners were on, the fire was out. Nearly blue with the cold, we ran for the cover of the blankets. No sooner did we reach the bed than we fucked again. At Larry's direction, I turned around on my stomach. He put two pillows under my stomach and *fucked me from behind. After Larry and I came, I turned around and nestled in his arms. I thought about the fire, and I felt warm and safe—and so we slept.*

How to Make a Bestseller

If anybody told me a year and a half ago that I would write a book, not only would I have laughed, but I probably would have called the person an idiot. But life works in strange ways, and here I was writing *My Life with Xaviera*.

When I delivered the completed manuscript to my publisher, he asked if I was willing to do a promotional tour to publicize the book.

Instead of thinking about what I was getting myself into, I blurted out, "Sure, I'll do exactly what Xaviera did. You make the appointments, and I'll do all the radio, TV, and newspaper interviews you can arrange." I'd put aside all my business interests and just concentrate on the book tour whenever they wanted me.

No more was said about it until just before the

book was due to hit the stands. I was told a coast-to-coast tour was set up for me. I would start in Florida, then fly west to Phoenix, Los Angeles, San Francisco, heading back through the Midwest and ending on the East Coast.

A week later a set of tickets were thrust in my hands, along with instructions, an itinerary, and hearty good luck wishes. I was given promotional items to present to the heads of the companies that would be distributing the book. They were navy blue ties embroidered with a silver fox and made especially for this trip. I also brought along a bunch of pictures of Xaviera and me.

As I drove to LaGuardia Airport to catch a flight to Florida, I was scared stiff. I had never appeared on a radio or TV show. It was too late now to back down. I relaxed into my seat and hoped for the best.

I arrived in Miami to be met at the airport by John, a field man for the book distributors. He would be showing me around town, and making certain I got to all the radio and TV appearances scheduled for me. He would introduce me to the wholesale distributor, and show me the warehouses where my books were stored. This was a most important part of the tour, since there I would meet the route men who would distribute the books throughout the city, refilling racks as the books were sold.

I checked in at the Marriott Hotel. After organizing myself, I called a good friend of mine named Vernon. We met at the hotel, and he and John and I had dinner together. Although I was loosening up a bit, I was still very apprehensive about "tomorrow."

My first date was a call-in radio show. I was forewarned that I'd meet a very, very tough M.C. who would probably eat me up and spit out the pieces. We met, and from that moment on I had no more trepidations about doing the other radio and TV appearances. He didn't have horns—as a matter of fact he was a nice guy. We sat there for two hours talking with people on the telephone. Strange as it seems, throughout the entire tour I never got any nasty questions or remarks from call-in people. The worst thing ever said was by an elderly man who wanted to know if Xaviera and I used mouthwash before we kissed.

I did a few newspaper interviews, one TV program, and then went on to St. Petersburg. In St. Petersburg I was again met by John. He took me to the Hilton Hotel for what turned out to be one of the most nightmarish experiences of my life. That weekend the Hilton was hosting the high school band competition for bands from all over the United States. There must have been forty or fifty bands housed in my hotel. As I got out of the car, I was greeted by a congregation of about a thousand kids hanging out in the lobby of the hotel. A few of them had instruments in their hands; some were playing them. Most of them were just standing there; the place was so crowded, they couldn't sit down. Through this swarm I walked—correction, squeezed—toward the elevator.

As the elevator started to climb, we stopped at every floor. The door opened on about fifty people standing there waiting for the elevator and another two hundred sitting in the hallway.

At the tenth floor I wiggled my way out of the elevator, but it was like an obstacle course to get to my door. For the next few days I had to allow an extra fifteen minutes to get from my room to the elevator, and another fifteen minutes to get to the lobby.

The first day there I met some newspaper people and had my first autograph party. I sat in a chair at a table in an enclosed shopping mall as people walked past, looking twice to see who I was. It was strange at first. But after a while people managed to warm up, and so did I. I took a whole bunch of books and scattered them over the mall floor. As people walked through, they saw the books lying there, but didn't know what it was all about. They tiptoed around them, and I would yell, "Why don't you pick one up, and I'll autograph it for you?" A lot of them started to do just that, and the fun began.

I noticed a very attractive young couple walking arm in arm down the mall. They looked at me, sidestepped the books, and then passed by. I noticed them because the woman was especially beautiful. About five minutes later she came back, picked up a book, and went in and paid for it. I asked her if she would like me to autograph it for her. She completely ignored me and left with the book.

I guess about a half-hour later her guy came back and bought a copy of the book. I asked him if he wanted me to autograph it, and he smiled and let me. I guess she had been afraid to say to him, "Why don't you buy that book? I'd like to read it," and he was as afraid to admit his interest. So, two people bought the same book, and I wonder if either one will ever know the other bought it. It's a shame people cannot relate to one another.

The next day John took me to the Tampa airport. I called New York and was given instructions to head to Jacksonville.

On arriving, I went to one of the airport guards and asked him to escort me to the press conference room set aside for my interview. As it turned out, there was only one young lady reporter there instead of the anticipated four or five. To be honest, I was just as glad. She was very lovely, and after we talked for about a half-hour, she took a few pictures. Glad of the female companionship, I checked my bag and we toured the airport. I bought her lunch and a couple of drinks. We shared a few laughs, and before I knew it, I was back in Miami, and it was still early afternoon.

This time I had to check into the Playboy Plaza

Hotel in Miami Beach. As I arrived at the desk, I knew I had been recognized. A few people behind the desk had my book, and asked me if I would please autograph it for them. Later I found out that when the reservations had been made at the different hotels, a letter of confirmation had been sent out, and a copy of the book was sent to the manager of each hotel. So here at the Playboy, not only did the manager have my book, but so did most of the guys and girls behind the counter. I spent about ten minutes autographing and then went to my suite.

Looking out the window, I decided it was still early enough to get some sun. I grabbed my bathing suit and raced down to the pool. The sun felt great. I must have been there for about an hour before it started getting cool. Picking up my towel, I headed back to my room to relax. I was getting a little bored, but figured a little rest would cure that.

As I opened my door, I was startled by what I saw. Sitting on the couch in the middle of the living room were two super-attractive young ladies—neither of them fully clothed. Although they wore little bikini bottoms, they were completely bare-chested! This wasn't St. Tropez yet!! Before I could react, they got up and walked over to me. As they approached me, I could feel their eyes looking through me. They introduced themselves as Darlaine and Peg. Peg walked over and put her arm around my waist, and Darlaine grabbed the little string at the front of my bikini bathing suit and gave a pull. I think I was still a little scared, but I had no intentions of fighting anyone, and in less time than it takes to say boo, my trunks were lying around my ankles. I felt it was only fair that I do the same to the girls, and as I pulled the bows on the sides of their suits, their bikini bottoms dropped to the floor. I didn't have a chance to ask any questions or to feel uncomfortable, as they put their inside arms around my waist, and with their free hands put their cool fingers over my cock and balls. I must say it was quite a sensation.

I think the fact that I was already partially undressed and had just come up from the pool added to the ease with which things started happening.

It was quite a while before we had a conversation. They escorted me back to the couch in the center of the room. Darlaine pushed me down, and Peg knelt in front of me. Darlaine sat with me on the couch and started to kiss me, and then took my head and guided my lips to her nipples. I felt like a bottle baby. While I was sucking away, Peg started at my toes, licking her way up the inside of my leg, slowly up past my kneecap, along the inside of my thigh, all the time working herself up toward home plate. She finally arrived—a bases loaded home run! I tried to stop her head from continuing on its journey, but happily there was no way I could do that.

Darlaine, in my arms, was now back kissing me with most of her body on top of my chest, and Peg started to lick my cock. Yes, it was at full mast, and about two and a half seconds later I came all over Peg. I didn't have a chance to warn her. I was embarrassed. I had pulled a booboo. I didn't let her know I was coming.

But! I don't think they were really shocked or disappointed that I came so quickly. They jumped up playfully, and while Peg was cleaning herself, Darlaine went to the bathroom and returned a few seconds later with a washcloth not too well squeezed out and playfully threw it at me.

While she was cleaning me, I had time to think about what had happened. It was sort of weird ... intercourse, well some form of it ... after only the briefest of introductions. Things like this usually don't happen ... or do they?

I looked at my two new friends and noticed they were both quite pretty. Darlaine was a dark-haired girl, her hair falling on her shoulders. She was very well proportioned, with a narrow waist. Peg was even more attractive. She was a pert blonde with short hair cut in a boyish bob and the most fantastic breasts I'd ever seen. Her body was a marvelous sight.

It seems like the whole hotel knew I was arriving, and Darlaine and Peg had been waiting for me in my room, since out of about fifteen kids they had won the right to rape me.

"Everyone was curious about you, and wanted

to know if Xaviera's stories were true," smiled Darlaine. "So we thought we'd just find out for ourselves."

I got up and went to the telephone and called room service for drinks. I went to the bathroom and got three bath towels. Putting one around myself, I threw the other two to the girls. "Please put these on, kids. I think I'll be a little more comfortable when room service arrives.

Soon the bellboy came. After signing the check, we settled down to have a few drinks and a bite to eat. About a half-hour later, I noticed none of us were wearing our bath towels, and my cock was in an upright position looking for trouble. Of course, the fact that they had both been sitting there playing with each other's breasts had nothing to do with it. Sipping my drink, I was watching them. I wanted to be part of their playing, so I got up from the couch and walked over to the club chair they both were sitting on. Bending down, I started to kiss Darlaine on the lips. She immediately took her hand and placed it on my erect penis. Both girls stood up, Peg sliding around behind me. Standing with her cunt touching my ass, she started to run her hands up and down my stomach. I turned around, put my arms around her, and gave her a kiss. While I was doing this, I felt Darlaine's hands trying to match my erect prick with Peg's cunt. It wasn't too hard a thing to do, and a few minutes later, with her legs around me, I was in her. Darlaine was right beside us. Her body was pressed against the two of us. She had one hand on my balls and with the other hand was manipulating Peg's cunt as my prick moved in and out. I could feel Peg shudder and knew she was coming. This time, however, I had control over my feelings, and I knew damn well there was going to be a lot more fun before I came.

I pushed Peg away and walked over to the couch. Tapping the cushion with one hand, I waited for someone to sit down next to me. Peg was the first one there, so I turned her on her knees with her head on her arms, which were resting on the arm of the couch. I knelt behind her and spreading the cheeks of her ass, I entered her cunt doggy style. I placed my hands over her breasts with her nipples between two fingers of each hand. I started a rhythm by which my cock and my hands seemed to be working together. Enjoying myself to the fullest, I took one hand from her breast and moved it down to her cunt where I felt her clit standing up like a nipple. I started to massage it between two fingers when I felt Darlaine's presence. She had her fingers about the cheeks of my ass and started to move them inward, kissing and hugging my ass cheeks all the while. If this continued, I knew I would come immediately. Yelling a little bit, I turned around and moved Peg from the middle of the couch, and put Darlaine in the same position Peg had been in, entering her the same way. We started to kid around, and I tried to do as many different positions as I possibly could, always stopping when I felt I might be coming.

I knew that both girls had come quite a few times. I could feel them both shudder a couple of times, and I had to hold back so the fun could continue. It was then that I felt I had given them a good time, and Xaviera's stories were defended.

Without a moment's hesitation I decided Peg was going all the way with me. I rearranged her on the couch. This time I placed the back of her head on the couch arm. I took one of her legs and put it on the top of the couch and put the other leg over my shoulder. I then lowered myself into her cunt. Her eyes opened wide, and small gasps escaped through her parted lips. I started to go very slowly, looking into her face. When she started to move her head back and forth in ecstasy, I pushed my prick hard inside her as her cunt closed around me and held me tight. I knew I was not going to be able to hold out much longer. I lowered my stiff arms and put them around her so that my head was right next to hers, and started a very gentle, but full rotation of my hips. Instead of just going up and down, I pushed myself all the way up and stopped, and then came back almost all the way out. With just the head of my cock in her cunt, I paused. Peg, looking at my cock held motionless in her beautiful cunt, let out a low moan, and I pushed myself all the way up, withdrawing slowly again. This time her hands reached for my hard prick. Her fingers encircled it and began exploring my warm wetness. Nimbly she moved a finger toward her clit and ran it around the place where we met. This woman was driving me wild. I repeated her action while she eagerly watched. She loved watching herself in a fuck, and this really turned me on. I inched my cock further up into her, and her cunt started throbbing.

For an instant my attention turned to Darlaine who was rubbing her cunt while watching us from the floor. I took her hand and placed it on my prick, which was still in Peg. She explored Peg and me until I knew we'd reached the point of no return. Returning to her own cunt, and my ass, she began shuddering in orgasm. Peg's cunt pulled on my prick, and I thrust myself deep inside her. Stars started exploding in my head. I was coming, bursting like a rocket inside Peg, while she shook with orgasm and Darlaine's dripping cunt was resting on my ass. Wow! The dam had burst.

I lay exhausted in Peg's arms, completely drenched with my own sweat. Fortunately, Peg didn't mind if I stayed in her, while Darlaine curled up between our legs.

After lying still in her arms for a while, I patted Peg, got up, and went into the bathroom to shower. When I finished showering, the girls took their shower, and we made plans for the evening. I asked if they'd join me for dinner, and I was very pleasantly surprised when they said yes. They didn't have to work that evening, and wherever I wanted to go, they would be only too happy to join me.

I called the La Parisienne Restaurant, a very lovely French restaurant, and about an hour later the three of us went to dinner.

When we finished eating, and I asked the girls to select a discotheque where we could go and do a little dancing. The girls couldn't seem to make up their minds where to go, so I took them to a discotheque that I like in Key Biscayne, called The Fiddler's Green.

We entered The Fiddler's Green and were given a small table near the band. The band was very good and consisted of about eight people. I danced with both girls for almost two hours.

Then we got into my rented car, and I started driving back to the hotel. Darlaine had become the boss. She asked Peg not to sit in the front with us. "Get in the back and stretch out." Peg jumped in the back, and Darlaine and I stayed in the front.

As soon as I pulled out of the driveway, Darlaine bent over as if she were going to put her head on my knee and go to sleep. But two seconds later, I realized she had no such intention, as I felt the zipper of my pants being opened. I put my hand in her bushy hair and pulled her away from me for a second in order to plant a kiss on her lips. I then allowed her to go back on her treasure hunt. She soon found out it wasn't that easy because I wore very brief bikini shorts, which have no opening. The only way she could gain access to my cock would be for me to take my pants and underpants off. I was curious to discover what she would do. I didn't have long to wait because I found out she was not about to be thwarted by my underwear. I raised my hip up while I felt her take my pants and underpants down. There was Junior standing at erect attention, waiting to be kissed and fondled. I would have loved to have the feeling last forever. After about five minutes, making sure my cock was well in her mouth, I came, and I held her head down very gently so that this time there would be no spillage. This time all of my juices would flow down her throat.

When she looked at me quizzically, I explained that the toll booth was a few minutes ahead, and I didn't want to have to stop in the middle.

Arriving back at the Playboy Hotel, I woke Peg up, and we trotted up to the suite.

Once inside, I became the leader. "Girls, don't you dare stop in the living room. Walk right through. Make a right-hand turn, and get into the bedroom.

It must have been about 2:00 in the morning. Peg and Darlaine started to take off their dresses.

I went into the bathroom to take a shower. As I showered, the bathroom door slowly opened and in walked the two girls. They opened the shower door and walked in beside me. It was a lot of fun being soaped down by two lovely girls. A little while later, three dried bodies once again entered the bedroom, and once again a session was about to take place. I was sure that when the girls got together with the rest of their friends the next day, they would tell them I had passed the course handsomely.

The next morning being Saturday, they had to be at work. So we woke early and said our good-byes.

I headed toward the Dinner Key to join my good friend, Vernon, aboard his boat, *The Libertine*. I got to Vernon's boat about 9 A.M. We spent about an hour shopping for soda and sandwiches. About 10 we headed out into the deep blue. We had been traveling about an hour or so at a very slow speed when all of a sudden another boat pulled up near us. It was an older boat. Vernon explained to me that this boat was owned by a close friend. These were some ex-friends of Xaviera, and their boat was often used for pornographic movies. Vern laughed as he said, "We all had things in common. Everyone fucked Xaviera."

"Tie up, I don't care." I thought it might be fun.

About fifteen minutes later we tied both boats together. It was a ticklish job, but Vern soon accomplished it. Once tied up, we went aboard to the much larger boat. Now Vern's boat was not small. It was at least fifty feet long. I would assume the other boat was at least seventy feet. It was built like the old-fashioned boats, with all sorts of staterooms upstairs and crew's quarters down below.

I stepped on this other boat and went to the wheelhouse, where I found two lovely, topless young ladies and was offered a drink. Five minutes later, I knew that I was aboard a boat full of swingers. All of the guys were good-looking and nice. But the girls were something else, each one a little more suntanned and beautiful than the next, and completely uninhibited. I wasn't on board more than five minutes when one of the guys suggested that I take one of the girls to a room and find out if she wasn't as good as Xaviera. It's a funny thing. I don't walk away from sex. The night before I had been lovingly trapped by two girls, and I enjoyed every moment of it, but here it was a cold and calculated arrangement. This didn't turn me on. As a matter of fact, it turned me off.

I asked Vern if we could get away, and cast off. He was a little surprised at my reaction, but after about five minutes he saw I was really sincere. He suggested we have one more round of drinks and then split. We sat down for our last drink, and I noticed that all the people were now walking around completely nude. A couple were sunbathing wearing nothing, and there was one girl sitting in the middle of a stateroom on her haunches, carrying on a conversation with a couple of guys on the only subject these people knew anything about—sex. I really wanted to leave, and Vern, noting my agitation, made his excuses, and away we went.

We took his boat just outside the Key Biscayne Yacht Club and anchored it. I jumped overboard and went swimming. After a few hours of sunbathing, we started back to the Marina. To this day, Vern never asked me why I backed off from a swing. As a friend, he acknowledged the fact that I wanted to split.

Vern dropped me off at my hotel after dinner, and I got a good night's sleep. The next morning I took a taxi to the airport, where I was to catch a flight from Miami to Phoenix.

By the Time I Got to Phoenix

I arrived in Phoenix about 11 A.M. I was picked up by a cowboy-type named Frank. He was wearing a rope tie, jeans, and a big hat. We were going to the Carefree Inn, which is outside of Phoenix in a town called Scottsboro, about an hour away.

The reason for my going here was twofold. A convention was being held by the book distributors (Independent News). These were the people who were responsible for seeing that my book got out on the stands. A year before when my book was only a passing idea, I had flown to the Playboy Club at Lake Geneva in Wisconsin to meet this group of guys. At that time we had talked about my writing a book and their giving me help. When I heard about this convention, I requested that the Publicity Department give me the right to go there and renew my friendship with these people. I knew if anything could make my book a success, their perseverance would surely help.

Publicity thought this was a great idea and arranged a full program of TV and radio stuff besides.

Arriving at the hotel, I met all my old friends from Lake Geneva. We all sat around the pool, talking and having a few laughs. They told me that I had just missed all the fun. Linda Lovelace had been in the hotel the day before to publicize her book. She had been quite a lot of fun, and I wondered what might have happened if the two of us had met.

I had an appointment to meet one of the newspaper reporters in the lobby. Excusing myself, I left, and about ten minutes later was met by Sue, a very pretty young lady of about twenty-three or twenty-four. Introducing herself, she proceeded to take some pictures of me in the lobby and in front of the building. The hotel itself was a madhouse. We looked for a quiet spot to sit and talk. Not being able to find any, I suggested that she come to my hotel room, if she didn't mind.

About five minutes later, we were sitting at opposite sides of the table, and I was talking into her tape recorder, answering the numerous questions she asked. We finished about forty-five minutes later, and I suggested a sandwich and a drink. I called room service, and the food and drinks were delivered. We sat around and ate, and I asked her if she would like to go for a dip. She said sure, but asked where could she find a bathing suit.

She was a big girl and stood about 5'10" or 5'11", every inch of her well proportioned. She had a wonderful figure. I don't know how it started, but in minutes we were in each other's arms lying on the bed. The first time we made love, we became acquainted, but the second time we made love, it was no longer an acquaintance. Very honestly, I often wonder if the next-door neighbors ever heard her screams. It was a warm, wonderful thing—the beginning of a nice relationship. For the first time since I started the tour, I felt I had met someone I really enjoyed, not just sexually, but as a human being. I suggested that we have supper together, and we did.

I no sooner got back to my room when all hell broke loose. A bunch of the executives from New York wanted me to go into town with them. They had already put a carton of my books in the car. I was to join them at a cocktail lounge. They wouldn't take no for an answer. So I looked at Sue very apologetically, and told her I would get back as soon as I could. She understood. As a matter of fact, I think she welcomed my leaving because it gave her a chance to catch a few extra winks. So after kissing her goodbye, I joined seven other people, and we went into town.

They took my books and put them in the middle of the large round table where we sat. Some of the fellows disappeared into the crowd, but most of us sat around the table boozing and telling jokes.

The place was full of young girls. Whenever one would walk past our table, one of the executives would yell out, "Meet the Silver Fox. He wrote this book. What's your name? Larry, autograph the book for this lovely girl."

When we'd run out of books, John would go out to the car to get more. I think the guys just wanted to enjoy themselves, and were not looking just to pick up girls—or were they? Anyway, it sure as hell started to get to me. I didn't like the whole idea. At one point when everyone's back was turned, I took about ten books and threw them on the floor under the table so no one would see them. I must have autographed about eighty-five books.

All of a sudden a very pretty girl came walking over to the table. I had seen her walk into the place earlier and remarked to Greg, who was sitting next to me, "If I had my choice of any girl, there's one I would really like to meet." She had heard I was in the restaurant—who hadn't?—and since she had been a friend of Xaviera's, she introduced herself to us. She was now going to college in Madison, and wanted me to let Xaviera know she had bumped into me. She joined our little party.

Henry picked up the check and insisted we go to another club. I wanted to get back to the hotel, for obvious reasons. But there was no way out. I couldn't take the car and leave the others stranded. Not only that, since I was somewhat of a celebrity, they all wanted me around. It had to be 2 A.M. when I finally dumped the last body at his hotel room door.

I went back to my room, where Sue was asleep. I didn't have the heart to wake her up. I let her sleep the night through. Early the next morning, I was awakened by her shaking me. She had overslept a little herself, and had to get to work. I quickly asked her for her office number and told her I would call her in the next hour or two, as soon as I found out what might be happening. I had a lot of shows to do during the day.

My chauffeur was the son of the owner at the Phoenix wholesaler, the Strong News Agency. A real nice kid. We made everything on time. Once we stopped in front of a large downtown office building so he could watch the girls take their lunch breaks. At nineteen years old he liked to watch "the girls go by."

That evening there was going to be a farewell banquet, as the next morning everyone was going home. A little later, I called Sue and told her if she would come back out, we would go for dinner in the main hotel and avoid the banquet.

She arrived back at my hotel at about 4:30. She walked into the room as if she had lived there her entire life, excused herself as she went into the bathroom and took a long shower. I walked over to her, put my arms around her, and gently kissed her.

We were lying on the bed in each other's arms for a few minutes when she asked, "Are you familiar with the warm water trick?"

Before I could answer, she got up, went to the bathroom, and returned with a mouth full of fairly warm water. She then took my cock and slowly eased it into her mouth. Feeling the warm water was a nice sensation, but what happened after was completely unique. With a slight manipulation of her lower lip, she allowed the water, drop by drop, to drip onto my balls. By the time her mouth had emptied, I was ready to explode, and I did.

About 6:00 the two of us got up, put on sport clothes and started for the hotel dining room. Unfortunately, we were seen by the others.

We stood talking and drinking at the bar, and Henry suggested that we join them for the banquet. Reluctantly, we both went to the banquet that night. Henry was the boss. He asked Sue if she would streak across the banquet hall! Wow, the look she gave me!

Shortly I'd have to leave for my flight to LA. Sue asked me please not to go without her. She was a little afraid of Henry. She drove with us to the airport, and I purchased a ticket for her, so she could join me next weekend. I kissed Sue goodnight, took off for Los Angeles and the Beverly Wilshire Hotel.

L.A., Olé ... Oh, Jane!

I became very much involved in the TV and radio interviews in Los Angeles. I felt I would be too tired to pursue my association with Sue. I called her and explained. I wanted her to cash in the ticket and buy herself a little gift. I was sorry, but I couldn't ask her to come to LA. She understood, but I was surprised two days later when I received a note from her.

> Dear Larry,
> Enclosed find the money from your ticket. You still have my phone number. If you're in Phoenix or Los Angeles again, please call me. I would like to renew our relationship. Thank you for a very enjoyable 30 hours.
>
> Sue

The Beverly Wilshire is a beautiful hotel, each floor designed in a different period. My floor was the 2001 era. All the furniture was exceptionally modern, but beautiful.

As soon as the bellboy left, I unpacked my luggage. It only takes a few minutes since all of my clothes are already on wire hangers. I pulled out the interoffice memo I had from Warners and started to make the necessary telephone calls.

The most important call I made was to Hank, a book reviewer for a local newspaper. I dialed his home number and got no answer—for the next three days.

I couldn't understand where he was. He had written to me in New York, and we had talked on the phone. He expected my call. I couldn't understand it. I left a message on his telephone machine, and said, "Fuck it!"

A few days before I was to leave for San Francisco, I got a panicky call from Hank. "Larry, I didn't forget our appointment, but I was away. I just got back from Acapulco with my girl."

"Hank, you are a pain in the ass. Do you know how often I called you?"

"I'm sorry. Please come over to my house, and I'll explain," he said.

Happily surprised, I told him I would be there in about fifteen minutes. I walked from my hotel to his apartment. Upstairs, I rang the bell and was ushered into the living room by an unbelievably beautiful six-foot-tall girl. She explained that Hank would be back in a few minutes. He had told her I would be there and I should make myself comfortable. Make myself comfortable! Who is kidding who?

Hank had tremendous throw pillows all over his living room. This girl immediately fell upon one, and, as she did, looked up at me with a smile. If it weren't that I was waiting for Henry, I suppose I would have sat on her pillow or on her. This girl was exquisite and had that "I dare you" look on her smiling face. We didn't talk much—it wasn't necessary. She had been walking around in a pair of bikini-bikinis. Seating myself in a living room chair, I fought down my hard-on.

I was interrupted as Hank burst into the room. He had run down to the store to purchase a few essentials in case I wanted a drink. Thanking me for coming, he explained where he had been. Just before I arrived in L.A., Hank got an invitation to go to Acapulco with his girlfriend whom I'd already met, a beautiful girl of about twenty-three or twenty-four. What made her even more stunning was that she was about 5'11" in her stocking feet. Hank said that as far as the interview for his paper was concerned, it would appear in the Sunday paper about two weeks hence. We sat down and finished the interview in about fifteen minutes.

As I got ready to leave his apartment, I again was pleased to hear Hank say, "Larry, what are you doing this evening? Let's all have dinner together."

"OK, Hank, why don't you and Jane join me at my hotel. After all, my publisher's paying for it. Let's have an evening on the house. It's 4:30 now. What do you say we meet at 7?"

A few minutes before 7 Hank called from the lobby. I joined him and Jane. We went to a very fine restaurant in the Beverly Wilshire and spent the rest of the night sightseeing in LA.

They took me up and down Sunset Strip, showed me all the things I had read and heard about over the years—Grauman's Chinese Theatre, The Brown Derby, as well as the Swinging Strip. We spent the whole evening running around, finally stopping at a few Pickwick Book Stores, where Hank introduced me to the manager and employees. We moved some of my books from the back to the main store entrance. I autographed a few books and had a lot of fun.

I said goodnight to Hank and Jane and suggested if they wanted to use the hotel swimming pool, I would leave my key at the front desk, and they could use my room to change clothes. I would be busy as I had a couple of TV appearances to make the next morning, so we said goodnight.

In the morning I met Ernie, a great guy, who, being the distributor's rep, took me over to Burbank, where I was going to the NBC studios to see about the "Tomorrow Show." We had lunch in the NBC cafeteria, and I had a very interesting conversation with one of the show's producers. We hit a few bookstores, and then at about 2 in the afternoon I was returned to my hotel.

I slowly went upstairs to my room. Arriving there, I realized there was someone's clothes spread on the bed.

"Anyone here?" I called out.

Then it hit me like a hammer—my offer of the night before came back to me. Couldn't be—I hadn't left any message at the desk. Never mind! I got out of my clothes, into my bathing suit, and down to the pool I went.

As I walked down the hallway and onto the terrace, I saw Jane lying on a chaise longue. She was wearing the same bikini of the previous day. We made small talk, but I knew what was on my mind. After about ten minutes of conversation and another ten minutes of swimming, I told her I had to go back to my room to make a couple of phone calls. Without asking her to join me, I asked if she would like a drink. She said yes. She gave me her order, and I left.

I knew Jane would not be long in following. When I got to my room, I hadn't even picked up the phone to call room service when in walked Jane. I picked up the phone and gave our order, while she walked into the bathroom.

A few minutes later I walked into the bathroom. Jane was standing there nude, sort of showing me her body as she pirouetted around. She didn't wait for me to make up my mind—she walked over and, like an expert, pulled the string on my bathing suit. Sliding my suit around my ankles, her mouth brushed past my now erect cock. I pushed her away and walked into the shower, and was immediately followed by Jane.

I don't know how many of you have ever had sex in the shower. It's a wonderful place. The soap is like an aphrodisiac that can really turn you on. Well-soaped fingers fit so easily in places that are normally difficult to invade. The soap allows all sorts of penetrations. Scrubbing her back and front, as her finger went up my rectum, I almost wanted to come, but didn't. Then as her hands played around with my chest and the inside of my legs, her fully soaped hand moved to my cock and began a rhythmic stroking. Not wanting to hold back I gently slid my cock in her cunt. It went in so easily.

Enough already! We left the shower to dry off.

While drying each other off, I wanted to hurry up and throw her on the bed. All of a sudden, there was a knock on the front door. Oh, shit! Of all times to have room service appear. Leaving Jane in the bathroom, I tried to pull a towel around me, but found that impossible and embarrassing. There is no way you can cover a flagpole with a towel. So what I did was the next best thing. Wearing nothing, I went to the door and opened it. As the bellboy walked in, I used the door as a towel. I pulled it open, and I covered myself with it. I told him to put the drinks down on the cocktail table. As he walked back into the hall, I closed the door behind him saying, "Wait a minute. I want to get your tip." I ran to my bureau where I got a couple of dollars, and, opening the door again, gave it to him. I turned around to find Jane standing behind me, laughing like an idiot—which is just how I felt.

She picked up her drink and offered me one. She was speechless looking at my body. Without any further ado, she came over, took me gently by the arm, and led me to the couch. Pushing me down, she spread my legs apart. Instead of sitting next to me, she put her knees on the floor and her head in front of my penis. Opening her mouth, she put my very hard cock into it, and I almost fainted. It was like it had been put into a deep freeze. Her mouth was freezing. I yelled, "Stop!"—too late. Seconds later, I came in her mouth. There was no way I could hold back.

Again I felt like an idiot—like a sixteen-year-old kid with his first trick. She had been so quiet because there were ice cubes in her mouth. When they had almost melted, she had put her mouth about me. What a sensation!

Jumping up, she started to laugh. What kind of stud was I not to know of the ice trick. The fact is, I knew all about it, but this was the first time it had been played on me when I didn't expect it.

When you expect a loving, warm mouth, and you find a freezing cold one—WOW!

I got up, still feeling like an idiot, and walked over to get my drink. I felt very guilty all of a sudden for having made it with this girl. First of all, Hank was my friend. Second, and most important, my girl was in New York waiting for me. I had this sudden recollection of how I used to feel waiting for Xaviera while she was fucking or sucking someone else instead of me. I rationalized quickly, appeasing myself with the fact that the girl was already there in my suite; I didn't pursue her. But it didn't work, I still felt guilty. What the hell! I could have learned something new to bring home, but I didn't. My girl knew what to do. This was no new trick to teach her. I figured I would have to wait another fifteen or twenty minutes, and then proved to Jane that I was really a man. Damn—I'll make her climb the walls. I am the master, and she is the student.

My mind was jolted by the ringing of the house phone. Hank was downstairs and could he come up. I stammered yes into the phone, slammed down the receiver, and quickly jumped into clothes. I made sure to put on a pair of underwear first. It would be very telltale if any dripping showed at the crotch. I actually had to force Jane to go into the bathroom to put her clothes on. She wanted to greet Hank in her birthday suit. When she saw how uptight I was about it, she went quickly into the bathroom as I went to answer the door.

If Hank didn't know what was happening already, I was sure he would as soon as he looked at my face. As I ushered him into the room, he seemed unaffected and sat down. He handed me a couple of books. They were the original Dell *Happy Hooker* books autographed by Xaviera. He told me the last time he saw her she had autographed the books for him, after a few hours in bed.

"Tell me, Hank, was she any good?" I asked. I opened each book, and there was Xaviera's handwriting, with one of her usual dedications.

He also showed me a few magazine articles he had done about Xaviera, with pictures I did not know anyone but me had. He said she had been in touch with him while in Canada and had mailed duplicates of the same photos to me.

We reminisced about a lot of people we both knew. After a while, we were acting like old friends.

Then he leaned over to me and said, "Larry, how did you like Jane?"

I almost fell off the chair. "What do you mean?" I asked.

Didn't you make it with her? She's all yours. I don't want her anymore. When we were in Acapulco and there were about a half a dozen Mexican guys hanging around, Jane was half dressed. She wore a mini with no panties. All the guys had the hots for her. Suddenly she disappeared. About 30 minutes later, she returned to tell me she had been raped by these six guys. She could have a case of anything in the world. I don't want her anymore. I told her to get out, and she thought she might live with you for a couple of days, at least until you leave L.A."

"Hank, you son of a bitch. You have got to be kidding. I felt guilty because I thought I did this behind your back. Why didn't you tell me about this last night? She could have something. What am I going to do if she does?"

"I don't know, Larry, but I just wanted to warn you."

When Jane came out of the bathroom, I could see the sheepish grin on her face, and I felt she knew I'd heard of her exploits. I suggested to Hank that we have a bite to eat downstairs, and asked him if he would wait for me in the lobby while I had a little conversation with Jane. I sat down with this laughing idiot and tried to talk to her while she tried to get my pants off so she could give me a blow job.

I made a deal with her. "Look, you and Hank seem to have split up. I'll be here for just another day and a half. Do me a favor. Go see a doctor. Have him check you out. If you check out, OK, no sweat. You can move in with me. When I go to San Francisco, you can go there with me. We'll see what happens after that. I might be going to Vegas as well."

She liked the idea and agreed to go to the doctor. A few minutes later, two smiling people, walking hand in hand, joined Hank for dinner. We had a light meal in the coffee shop. All I had was a hamburger because I was pretty upset, to say the least. Jane told me she was going back to Hank's apartment to get her clothing. I would let her do anything at that point as long as she would go to a doctor.

The next day I got up early in the morning and started on my round of meetings with Ernie. I was preoccupied all day. At about 11 A.M. I called Jane and got no answer. I tried again at 12. No answer again. I got a little panicky. Finally at 1:00 she answered the phone with, "I passed. I really passed. The smear test was in our favor. I'm clean. When can we meet?"

"Jane, I'm working today. I won't be done with these people until about 6 or 6:30. Give me a number where you're going to be, and I'll call you at 6 and we'll get together." I hung up feeling as if I were walking on air.

About 7 that evening I called the number Jane had left me. She answered, but I immediately hung up. At about 8 I called again, and this time a guy answered.

"Is Jane there?"

"Is this Larry?"

"Yeah, why?"

"Jane left a number for you to call her at. She

68

couldn't wait here any longer, so she went over to Bill's house. You can call there."

"OK, but in case I miss here, tell Jane I'm going to be tied up tonight—that an unexpected business meeting has come up. I'll call her as soon as I get done with my tour tomorrow. Thanks."

I hung up, and as you can well imagine, I didn't call her that evening or the next morning. The girl was just too much.

The Frisco to Vegas Roadrunner

The next morning I boarded a plane for San Francisco. In San Francisco I checked into the Mark Hopkins Hotel. It reminded me of the Plaza in New York.

San Francisco is a beautiful place. There are cable cars, pastel-colored houses, and flower-lined streets, Chinatown, and the Golden Gate Bridge, but there is also a feeling about being there—just about being alive in San Francisco. It was great.

I did quite a few radio and TV shows, went down to Fisherman's Wharf, and took the trolley cars all over town. The temperature there was about 60 degrees. The other cities I visited had temperatures in the 80s. I am a sun worshipper, so I was really anxious to finish my work and move on to a warmer climate. I was in San Francisco during the "Zebra" killings. The morning I arrived, a young man had been killed while unloading his station wagon. I think he was number ten. Everyone looked over their shoulders while walking the streets. This scared me also.

I decided to go southeast to visit Las Vegas, and combine business with pleasure. Ernie would meet me there and introduce me to the Vegas wholesaler. Now, trips to Las Vegas for me were usually gratis. Being somewhat of a gambler, I am pretty well known to most casino/hotel owners, managers, and pit bosses.

Reputable gamblers like myself—those who pay losses—are comped into hotels and allowed to sign markers at the gambling casinos. "Comp" means hotel accommodations are free, all hotel services—food, rooms, valet service, and so on.

Markers are forms of promissory notes that a gambler signs in various amounts. The gambler owes the casino money against these markers if he loses. If a gambler wins, he simply buys his markers back from the casino.

Only bona fide gamblers are "comped in"—those recommended by the regulars of Las Vegas.

I was comped in at MGM Grand Hotel, the newest and largest hotel in Las Vegas. It was ... a city within a city.

My suite was high up in the hotel, a suite usually assigned to "high rollers."

Although I'm not classified as a high roller—as a matter of fact I tend to be a bit conservative in my betting—I was given this extra courtesy due to the publicity I was receiving on my book.

The bedroom of this three-room suite had a huge round bed on a raised platform. Mirrored ceilings over the bed gave me the feeling of grandeur and decadence.

"Too much," I pondered, "but I'm here to rest, sun, and play games, so what the hell?!"

I jumped into a cool shower and prepared myself for a run at the crap tables, dinner, and maybe a return trip to the casino, especially if Lady Luck was with me. Lady Luck could be an expensive date—a very unpredictable lady, but one few men forget.

Now I've been told I'm a flamboyant and colorful gambler at the tables. I couldn't care less how I appear to others as long as those dice keep rollin' up the numbers for me!

I bought my usual allotment of chips and bet rather lightly while others rolled the dice, waiting for my turn. I casually scanned several people surrounding the crap table, especially an Oriental-looking woman bedecked in the most exquisite carved jade jewelry I have ever seen. The pendant she wore was jade surrounded by diamonds, with earrings, bracelets, and ring to match.

One of the casino's pit bosses, an old friend, noticed my interest in this exquisite-looking woman whose skin was like alabaster, starkly contrasted against coal black eyes. Her graceful, cool manner impressed me even more as she bet black $100 chips. Each time she won on a dice roll, she'd coolly pick up her pile of chips with her long, slender, well-manicured hands, fondle the chips a bit, and place them in the stacking bin provided for each player.

My pit boss friend nodded to me and half smiled as if to say, "Not bad, eh?" I was told this lady had entered the casino alone, was betting alone, and was *winning* alone.

I, too, was winning, but still waited for my roll at those hot dice. My turn came. I rolled. I rolled again, and again—and again.

For you nongamblers, the longer you roll the dice, the more you're apt to win. And I won! Did I ever?! I had a run of luck you wouldn't believe. Then came the seven and, baby, that's craps. A gambler must know when to quit. I knew my time was "Now!" My instinct, winnings, and hunger told me so.

As I cashed in my chips at the cashier's cage, a voice behind me said softly, "And I thought *I* was running lucky." It was the Oriental-looking lady. She was smiling now and looked less uptight than she had at the gaming table.

"The dice were sure with me tonight," I said as I stashed the wad of bills into my pocket.

"Why don't you put that money in the hotel safe?" my new-found friend asked.

"Naw, it'll be gone before the night's over," I answered. "I'll go back to the tables after dinner and probably give it all back."

"I haven't had dinner yet either. May I join you?"

"Why not?" I invited. "What is your food preference?"

"Something light—not too exotic."

"Let's dine at the French restaurant right here at the hotel, OK?"

"Fine," she said, as she took my arm and aimed me toward the dining room.

There was something strange about this woman, I thought to myself. She's extremely attractive but plastic-like. She moves slowly, yet she seems to be no more than in her early thirties.

We dined and talked. Midway through our dinner she told me she knew who I was, had read my book, and proceeded to ask me many questions about Xaviera. We talked about my book as well as about Xaviera. I told her that I had written the Nancy and the Transvestite stories, in a collection of letters to Xaviera.

Anxious to show off my fancy hotel suite and have some fun in that king-size bed, I glanced at my dinner companion and noticed, strange though she might seem, the young lady looked interested. A few drinks later I suggested we take a rest before returning to the gambling tables. She thought a drink in my room would be fabulous. So off we trotted.

This woman's enthusiasm was amazing me.

She seemed too willing, but I decided to dispel any fears and enjoy whatever she had to offer.

In the hotel room she seemed a bit reluctant to take off her clothes. Maybe she was a classy chick who wasn't used to this kind of pickup. But when I headed for the shower, she did not follow, and I got highly suspicious.

Donning a bathrobe, I returned to the living room to help her relax. The plastic look of this woman was becoming increasingly disconcerting, and finally I just asked why she was still dressed. Sliding my hand up her thigh, and reaching between her legs, I needed no answer.

I leaned back. "You cocksucker! You got five seconds to do the mile, heels and all, out of this hotel. Now!"

"It" got up and, very slowly shaking his hips, left. I was furious. Not really at him, but at me. *Damn!*

Lovely Las Vegas. Ernie took me to the University of Las Vegas. Lovely, suntanned kids at a lovely school. On campus there was a tremendous book store. Kids relaxed in small groups all over campus. I wished my kids were there. It was an experience. But for all the fun and lying in the sun, and making a tour of the different hotels to see if my books were there, I decided it was time to get back to New York City.

Early Sunday morning I caught a flight that brought me back to New York and to my girl.

I had a lot of good memories, but I wanted to be home. In St. Louis when I went looking for my book in some of the stores, the proprietor told me, "Yes, I have *My Life with Xaviera*, but it's going to cost you $2." They didn't have it on display. Believe it or not, they were selling it under the counter.

I went back once more to Las Vegas where I appeared on some great shows.

In Erie, Pennsylvania, I had a wonderful host and hostess. We made all the shows and the large sign of the Holiday Inn said "Welcome Silver Fox."

In Detroit, Charley, Stoney and Jr. were great. Richard made sure I missed no stores that carried my book.

In St. Louis, Mark took me to all my stops as well as "Your Place," a great cocktail lounge. I did one TV show three times. Helluva city.

In Washington I went to the Book Fair, signed books and visited the wholesalers. Ken introduced me to Jose. I look forward to seeing him again.

Did I leave out Sam at Dade County? He told me the story of how he originally ordered only 200 copies of *The Happy Hooker*, yet reordered 100,000 over the years. Somebody must be reading down there.

In Philly there is a great Italian restaurant that Abe took me to with Don. What an operation! Immense. It is here that I really saw some intelligent and aggressive bookselling.

In Chicago I autographed hundreds of books at Levy's (can't return 'em that way). One story that's worth repeating: I asked a middle-aged lady if I could autograph my book for her; she looked me in the eye and said, "I am sorry, sir, I don't read that type of book. Thanks anyway." What a beautiful lady.

How about Bob who loaded up his car to personally bring 500 books to a distributor at Hauppauge, L.I. That's dedication. (And a commission, too, I guess.) Let's see, at 15 cents a book in royalties for me, that's $75. Thanks, Bob.

I could go on forever. Everyone in the book business has been great, salesmen, jobbers, the distributor, bookstores—even some of the book reviewers. They can be sexy, too, you know.

The only other part of my tour that is particularly memorable is when I went to Canada. I stayed in Toronto for nine days. Long articles were written about me in all the newspapers, and I appeared on all the radio programs that it was possible to be on, thanks to Silvia Train, my P.R. lady. I once again renewed the friendships of Xaviera's ex-friends, and we had a lot of fun. We traveled all over and did a lot of things together. Richard and his wife Carol, drove me all over.

I paid Xaviera a visit on her birthday, actually the night before. We spent about three hours together. I took one of her ex-boyfriends along, young Gary, who now was a good friend of mine, but had been her companion in Acapulco. She gave me a hug and a kiss. We sat and talked and created a little furor in the cocktail lounge of the Hyatt Regency where I took her for a few drinks.

She looked at me with her green eyes, and kissed me on the cheek—or shall I say on the lips? —and made no comment whatsoever.

Gary and I then got up and left. She asked me to come to her party the next day. I told her I didn't think I could, but would think about it. I told her I thought it would be great to remain friends, close friends. But the next morning I was shaken back to reality when I was sitting with a newspaper reporter, giving him an interview for a Sunday supplement, and he called up Xaviera to get a little additional material, saying, "Xaviera, this is the *Toronto Sun*. We hear your ex-boyfriend is in town. What do you think? He's up here to plug his book. Do you have any comments?"

I was horrified to hear her say, "That book is terrible. It's really a bad book, and I'll tell you something else. I'm only getting 20 or 30 percent of his book. I should be getting 50 or 60 percent. You know, ever since I've known him, I guess he must have been what people say he is—a pimp— because he's always ripping me off."

When I heard this, I told the reporter not to suppress it. Print it, but please leave out her statement about my book being bad. He could do whatever he wanted with the rest of it. If any of my readers would care to have a photocopy of this article, I'd be only too happy to send it to them, because it was from that point on I realized there was no way to continue a relationship with Xaviera. Somewhere along the line she would have to learn that the old adage, "Don't tell me what you did. Tell me what you're going to do" is not always true. *C'est la vie!*

When I returned to New York, I called her lawyer, and told him, "From here on in, Xaviera's on her own. I don't want to become involved with any of her problems."

I had told Xaviera the night before when we sat hand in hand that there was no use in our fighting because whatever happened in an emergency, I would be the only person in the world to fly to help her. I wonder if that's true now.

The next day I went to the CBA. The CBA is the Canadian Book Association to which people come from all over Canada to see what books are being offered.

Before I had agreed to go, while I was still in New York, I had spoken to my publisher and told him that I didn't like the idea of going there to autograph books if Xaviera was going to be doing the same thing. After all, her book was just coming out then, and mine had already been out for two months, and I really didn't think it was fair for me to take some of the limelight away from her. He said to me, "Larry, I'm asking you to come because we want you here. We do not want Xaviera. She's not invited.

I spent the entire day at the CBA, had a great time autographing at least two or three hundred books for all the different people who wanted a copy.

That evening I said goodbye to some wonderful friends I had met in Canada. The next morning I did some shopping. The shops in the Yorkville section are fantastic. I bought a couple of suits at the House of Mann, and came back to New York so much happier for having finished the trip. Thanks, Sylvia.

Cock-a-bye Baby

It was so good to have Larry back. Being without him, while he was out promoting the book, was a trying experience. At night, alone in my apartment I longed to be in his arms, his beautiful cock inside me. I knew he'd be home soon, and slowly I accepted the waiting. Now, I could have been like Xaviera and fucked every guy around while he was gone, but after Larry, I knew sex with anyone else would be all wrong. The love and caring would be missing, and without that, sex is nothing.

It was a cold, snowy night in early February. Larry had been back about a week, and we went to a party in a Greenwich Village loft. One of those happy wine and cheese parties. We had a great time mingling among people there—the hip, the gay, the so-called sophisticated.

The host and hostess of the party were charming. He was a dark, handsome Italian, and Kim, his wife, a Eurasian beauty. Rock music was blasting as rainbow-colored strobes flicked to the frenzied beat.

People were super-friendly. One guy in particular, Ted, did his best to make everyone comfortable. Knowing Larry and Xaviera when they were together, he was so excited to meet me—the new woman in Larry's life. Later Ted introduced me to a few people and at one point he said, "This is the girl who is reforming Larry." "Fuck that, Ted," I said indignantly, "I don't intend to reform Larry or anyone else. Larry's great as he is, especially in the sex department. Furthermore, he says I'm better than Xaviera ever was—in and out of bed."

"Really!" Ed said, excitedly. "Kiss me!" he chided.

We both laughed and hugged each other.

A quiet, Haitian chick sat in a corner, slowly sipping her wine and looking shyly about the huge room. I felt sorry for her, since she spoke no English. Although she had come to the party with a stunning Frenchman, he had abandoned her.

Ted spied her the same moment I did, and realizing her awkward situation, ran across the room to her and sat down beside her.

I watched Ted flatter this beautiful lady with his fine French and continental charm. That was his way, and it was really nice. Soon the girl was smiling and perfectly at ease.

People kept entering the loft. Some stag, some escorted. One chap entered the semidarkened loft, greeted everyone, and walked toward our section of the room. It wasn't until his coat was off that I realized this was a woman. She was tall with extremely short, cropped hair—almost a crew cut. She reminded me of a fashion drawing—the long body, the small, short-cropped head.

Then I spotted a very attractive model whose husband is quite gay. She and "he" go to parties with his lover. Quite a trio. They do, I must say, look magnificent as they make their "entrance." Very fashion-conscious, the three of them are bedecked in the finest up-to-the-minute fashions, not only in clothes but in make-up and hairstyles. Make-up, of course, belonging to the legitimate "she.") Simone is French and her husband, Franco, is of Italian extraction. They met at the Pines on Fire Island. Simone loved Franco very much and Franco wanted a child. They were married and Simone gave Franco a beautiful son. Mission accomplished, Franco then resumed his gay love affairs and then there were three (sans baby) to make the round of parties.

Denim rubbed elbows with velvet and glitter at the party. Conversations started up spontaneously all over the room. Everyone was extremely friendly. The party was in full swing.

Larry and I were the first guests to leave. Happy people danced in the living room, imploring us to stay, but we were anxious to be alone.

Heady with wine, we walked the white streets of New York. It had stopped snowing by this time and the city was as deserted as a ghost town. Quiet, clean.

Silly and giggly, we made our way back to my apartment, lit a fire, and listened to some relaxing music. After a while, Larry decided to take a hot bath and "maybe" hit the hay. Usually, when Larry was soaking in a hot tub, I would join him. I'd often eat Larry under water. The warm water in the tub and in my mouth combined with the sound and feel of the bubbles was one thing Larry really enjoyed. His eyes closed, he'd just sit back and enjoy his "bubble bath."

"Is this a 'first'?" I'd ask later on.

"It sure is!" Larry would exclaim. "It was great!"

There were so many "firsts" that I often wondered what the hell Xaviera knew about lovemaking. I would often improvise spontaneously while making love to Larry. I wanted to do everything to please him.

Mesmerized by the fire and the music, I hadn't realized Larry had already left the tub and gotten into bed.

"You rat!" I said as I walked into the bedroom. "You didn't wait for me!"

Larry smiled lazily as I flung back the bedcovers. I hovered over him for a moment and gently made my way down to his cock. I ate him gently.

Larry was so tired. I knew he felt rather guilty about my eating him, and his not being able to reciprocate.

"Stop, you bitch, and get up here," Larry said, his body responding to my warm mouth.

"Come in my mouth," I mumbled, as I manipulated his big cock with one hand, my wet lips encircling it, while fondling his balls with the other hand, and putting a wet fingertip up his ass.

Larry sent his liquid into my mouth with such force, and I had his cock so far in my throat, that I swallowed him in one beautiful gulp.

I rose slowly and got a wet, hot washcloth from the bathroom, along with a dry towel. I gently washed Larry's beautiful genitals, dried them and smothered them with soft, gentle kisses. I pulled the blankets over us.

"Goodnight, my love."

We slept.

Taking the Baths with Erika

The days were growing short for Xaviera in America, and we were trying to make the most of the evenings we had left together. Xaviera's publicity tour was over, and her first book was going into a new printing each month. There were always flurries of hope that Xaviera would actually not be deported, and now I know she made her first big mistake when she didn't contest the deportation order, but back then we were intent on sharing as much time together as possible.

So one day, when Xaviera received a call from Erika, a close friend, my initial reaction was to not be interested in whatever Erika had in mind. I wanted us to have a lot of fun, and many nights to remember after we separated. I may sound sentimental, but I felt a deep relationship was about to be interrupted, if not terminated.

However, what Erika had in mind seemed like a fine way to spend an evening. She wanted us to join her and a few friends to spend an evening at the Continental Baths. I wasn't sure what the Continental Baths was all about, but it seemed to me I'd read about it in gossip columns. In any case, there was entertainment, and the Baths were famous for starting many great stars on their way. So I readily agreed to an evening at the Continental Baths.

That night we met at Erika's, and I had my first misgivings. I knew Erika from some parties, and knew about her sexual proclivities, mostly women, occasionally men, but still I was surprised to see that her escort for the evening, Saul, and two friends of his were all very gay. My initial reaction to the entire scene was barely masked hostility. I was the only straight person there.

These three men were all very good company, interesting, bright, fun to be with, and gentlemen in every sense of the word. They were very sympathetic about Xaviera's plight with Immigration, and the advice they gave was sincere. One of them was a lawyer, and he insisted that she should go to court to fight the deportation proceedings. His reasoning sounded logical, I had to admit, but it seemed to me he was ignoring the tens of thousands of dollars it would take to fight the government.

While we were having drinks, prior to going over to the Baths, the conversation turned, quite subtly as it happened, to sexual preferences. These guys were all gay, and it was no secret that Erika and Xaviera had made it together on more than a few occasions. I began to take a lot of kidding because I was the only "straight."

Things could have taken a nasty turn, but they didn't because the banter was good-natured and never malicious—none of that "You just don't understand us" crap, but a lot of interesting conversation.

We touched on everything from the right of homosexual couples to adopt children, to editorials in the *New York Times*.

On the way over there Saul explained to me what the place would be like. The Continental Baths is really a health club located in a famous landmark hotel on Broadway in the Seventies. It is strictly for men, and is frequented, so far as I could tell, strictly by homosexual or bisexual males. No "rough trade" here—the members are mostly mature men and a very sophisticated group, including writers, artists, owners of art galleries, boutiques, and the like.

The club occupies two floors of the hotel, and what makes the Continental Baths unique is that quite apart from being a health club equipped with all the usual facilities—gym, swimming pool, sauna baths—it also includes a kind of nightclub. Bette Midler, for instance, got her start there, and this evening, we were going to hear another new entertainer. So the Continental Baths is also a hot house for important new talent.

On Saturday night, and only on Saturday night, Saul said as we parked near the hotel, the club was "open to the public"—in other words, women were allowed to attend. The admission price for nonmembers on these "open" evenings was five dollars, which in effect was a cover charge, and not much different than a lot of nightclubs.

We arrived at the Baths, paid our admission fee, and were directed into a tremendous room that included a gymnasium, a swimming pool, plus the entertainment area in one corner. Coming from the cold March night into this place was like entering a blast furnace. At first glance this giant room seemed to be filled with guys walking around with towels around their waists, but Saul led us over to the area in front of the stage, where there were tables and chairs. I didn't see where there was any room for five of us to sit down, and from the glances and looks we were getting, I didn't feel the girls and I were very welcome. However, Saul, Jay, and Rex went around greeting their friends, and out of nowhere three chairs appeared for us. Some of the guys shifted tables, and soon the five of us were able to be seated at the same table. Only then did I realize that our three friends and I were the only fully dressed men in the room. A few of the men at the tables were completely nude—no towels, just their birthday suits!

Before I could reflect very much on this—and decide whether or not I felt uncomfortable in the midst of this nude homosexual crowd—it was time for the show.

The performance was good. The songs were lively, and everyone seemed to enjoy the singer. She had good style and a great voice. I wondered if I was viewing the birth of a superstar.

When the show was over, she got a lot of applause from the gay audience, and the five of us spent a few minutes discussing the act. Erika didn't care for her at all, she said, but the general feeling among the rest of us was that she was certainly talented.

Erika was also complaining about the heat. It was uncomfortably warm in there—so I got up and went over to the bar to get us some soft drinks. When I returned to our table, Erika had unbuttoned her blouse and pushed it off her shoulders. Her two big boobs were jutting out for all the world to see. Xaviera had unbuttoned a few buttons at the top of her dress, but nothing was showing except a little flesh below her neck. I wasn't aware that anyone at the other tables had noticed Erika's bare frontage, but a few minutes later when, still complaining about the heat, she took her blouse off completely, I could hear some angry conversation around us. I heard one guy say, "What's that bitch trying to do?" and another grumbling, "Who's the cow with the big tits?" There was some definite resentment toward Erika being bare to the waist.

Xaviera and I got up to walk around. On the way I suggested to Erika that she put her blouse back on. "OK, I hear you," she said, but showed no signs of heeding what I said. I wasn't going to make an issue of it—she wasn't *my* date—and I walked off with Xaviera.

When we returned to our table, Rex and Erika weren't there, but Saul and Jay were having what appeared to be an intimate conversation. But when we sat down, Saul said to Xaviera, "Hi, did you see much of the place?"

"Some," she said.

Saul looked at his watch and said, "You're lucky there's another show tonight. Shall I give you a guided tour of the rest of the place in the meantime? Would you like to do that? The show won't start for at least a half-hour."

That sounded fine with us, and we got up with Saul. Jay was already deep in conversation with a guy at the next table, but he waved at us and said, "See you later."

The Continental Baths is really a big YMCA without regulations. There are about nine hundred "hotel rooms" for rent at fifteen dollars a night, or for however long these gents want to spend doing their thing. These so-called rooms are really cubicles, both large and small, where a certain amount of privacy can be enjoyed. If guys wanted company, they left their doors open. Just don't make too much noise having your run—because there are "rooms" without ceilings. The only furniture of note in each cubicle is a big double bed. Probably nothing else is needed.

In addition there were two orgy rooms and an exhibition room for those who wanted center stage. The steam room was called the "Tunnel of Love."

Xaviera was not allowed to go above the main floor. "Larry, you can if you want," Saul said with an inviting smile. Xaviera insisted I go up, so I agreed apprehensively.

There were lots of occupied rooms, and lots of them had open doors. I couldn't resist taking a look, but as I watched two guys sucking each other off, I wanted to leave. Had Xaviera been there, she would have died, both of these guys had the hugest cocks I'd ever seen. I wasn't turned on, but I knew Xaviera probably would have joined right in. A guy with a good, big cock could win Xaviera's heart without even trying.

I told Saul I wanted to leave, and we did. Downstairs again, we were also given a tour of the shower rooms, the immaculate bathrooms, and the small kitchen facilities.

As we were returning to catch the next show, there was a lot of commotion coming from the pool area, where guys surrounded it three and four deep. We had to shove our way through to see what was going on. I had a sneaking suspicion I might know who was causing some of this commotion, and I wasn't disappointed.

There was Erika, completely bare-assed, accompanied by a lot of bare-ass guys, swimming up and down the pool, while all around the pool guys were cheering her on. It was like a scene out of some Esther Williams movie, except old Esther always wore a bathing suit.

I saw Jay a few feet away and managed to work my way through the cheering throngs to his side. I had to practically yell into his ear to make him hear me. "What the hell happened?" I asked him.

"Well, the manager came over to our table and asked Erika to put her blouse back on," he yelled back. "She did so, but you could tell that it pissed her off."

"Then what happened?"

"I don't know. I went over to the bar to get a Coke, and when I came back, she was gone. The next thing I knew, she was in the pool with all her fans!"

I didn't know who the manager was, but there were three guys completely dressed by the side of the pool, trying to grab hold of Erika and drag her out, so I figured he must be part of that group. Two of the guys were very, very big. The smaller one who I guessed to be the manager looked the unhappiest. The other two guys just looked very tough and very annoyed. They were professional muscle for those occasions when a little force is in order, and here they were with a nude broad shaking the whole place up. They couldn't jump into the pool and slug her, not with all her fans surrounding the pool, and they couldn't get hold of her to pull her out as "gently" as possible.

The manager and his two cohorts kept racing around the pool, but every time they got close to Erika, she'd push herself off one of the walls of the pool and swim away. If it hadn't been such a crazy and potentially explosive situation, I would have had time to admire her swimming style. Good breast stroke. Good back stroke, too.

As she swam by me, with the manager and his twosome still on the other side of the pool, I yelled to her, "Hey, Erika, over here!"

She heard me and detoured over to where I was kneeling by the side of the the pool. "What the hell do you think you're doing," I said to her, "training for the next Olympics?"

"That bastard made me put my top back on at the table, where it was so hot—and everyone else was allowed to be nude and comfortable—so I decided, fuck'em, there's only one way to cool off in this place, and that's in the pool. So I pulled off my top and my shirt and everything else, too, and here I am—having a great time. How do you like my fan club?"

Just then, out of the side of my eye, I could see the manager and his two companions approaching. Erika saw them too and pushed off toward the middle of the pool.

The manager, realizing that I had something to do with Erika, charged up to me and said, in a very unpleasant voice, "Look, mister, you've got to get that person out of the pool and into her clothes—she's undermining the morale of the place."

Playing dumb, I replied by saying, "I don't understand what's bothering you—everyone seems to be having a good time. Just listen to those cheers..."

"I hear them all right," he said. He then explained to me that when the Baths first opened, he'd had a difficult job getting the guys who came there to behave themselves in public—what they did in private was their business—but a little act like Erika's could tear the place apart. "I don't want this to get out of hand," he added, a bit menacingly, "so please ask your friend to leave the pool. Okay?"

"Okay," I responded. He was right, of course, because this was a private club, and women were allowed here only to see the show—and certainly not to *be* the show.

"Hey, Erika," I yelled at her, "get out of the pool. They're going to call the police!"

So far as I knew, this was a complete lie, but the important thing was that she agreed, after

95

thinking about it for a minute or so. Half a second later, there were ten towels around her.

"I think we had better get out of here," I said to both Erika and Xaviera.

"She can't go out in the cold right away," argued Xaviera. "Her hair is wet and ... she can't even put her dress on right away. We have to wait at least until she's all dried off." I got the distinct impression that Xaviera was proud of Erika for what she'd done.

The show was starting, so most of the guys around the pool were drifting back to their tables, and I went back too, while Xaviera took Erika into one of the dressing rooms and helped her dry off. Five minutes later they rejoined Saul, Jay, and me at our table, the two of them laughing and giggling like schoolgirls who'd snuck out after hours and were now terribly pleased with themselves for not having been caught. Then we all just sat and relaxed and enjoyed the show. However, the second the show was over, the manager and his two friends were by my side, inviting us to vacate the premises.

"I have complete respect for you and Miss Hollander," he said, "but I can't tolerate the behavior of your friend." Or words to that effect. I was busy getting us out of there, with Xaviera complaining that Erika's hair was still quite damp, and she'd catch her death of cold.

Five minutes later we were out on the street— the guys had decided to stay behind, which was perfectly understandable. Erika with her wet hair, and Xaviera and I with red faces, called a cab. Although I found it embarrassing, I think Xaviera secretly thought the whole thing was a great little adventure.

In the car Erika and Xaviera kept babbling away, which only made me angrier, and they started playing with each other's tits, which made me angrier still. And I decided to stay mad as hell at them the rest of the evening.

Which is too bad, in a way, because when we got back to Erika's, she and Xaviera began to make it with each other, and I wanted ... oh, how I wanted to jump in between the two of them.

But I didn't indulge in a three-way sandwich because I wanted to show them I was still mad.

In December of last year there was a cover story on Bette Midler and the story quotes her as saying, "At the Continental Baths I was playing to people who are always on the outside looking in."

That's just the way *I* felt sitting watching Xaviera and Erika.

How Do You Massage a Silver Fox?

Xaviera and I were spending a lot of time and money trying to forget she would be leaving the country soon. The time was drawing near, and whenever Xaviera wasn't off on a publicity tour, we relaxed and had a good time in New York— dinners, parties, evenings on the town, whatever struck our fancy.

One weekend I got a call from a friend of mine named Lou, a fellow junketeer to Las Vegas. It's odd how some friendships are. I think I saw more of Lou in Vegas than I did in New York, but he now had a suggestion for an offbeat evening in Manhattan that appealed to me.

"Hey, Larry," Lou said after the usual Hello, how are you? "how would you and Xaviera like to go to a massage parlor?"

"Why, you got a coed massage parlor in mind?"

"No, seriously—I belong to this place, a club. Where couples come together all the time."

"What do the girls get out of it—a lesbian experience?" I asked. So far this idea didn't much appeal to me.

"No, dummy. That's not the way it is at this place. This isn't one of those one-hour-to-get-your-rocks-off places. It's a really classy place where you go to spend the evening. You go swimming, have a few drinks, and some time during the course of the evening you get a massage."

"And what happens when you get a massage?"

"That's up to you. There are no rules about what can go on in the massage rooms, but this is a completely respectable place."

"OK, it sounds like fun. I'll ask Xaviera if she wants to go."

Ha, ask Xaviera if she'd like to be one of a few females among a small army of guys—I knew the answer before I asked. Her eyes lit up like Times Square on New Year's Eve.

That night, Lou, Xaviera and I arrived at his massage club, which was located in a large apartment building on West 57th Street. A pretty young woman asked to check Lou's membership card at the door. He explained to us that cash couldn't be used to pay for any of the regular services here. We were his guests, and he would sign for everything. The club would send him a bill at the end of the month.

Lou then led us to a large dressing room with lockers, where we would strip down to the altogether. I was suddenly glad for my nudist camp training. We could wear our towels to the pool, but swimming was in the nude. This was a club rule.

"Don't worry," he said, "it's all very relaxed here."

"Who's worried?" Xaviera said, flashing that famous lascivious grin of hers.

Lou told us we'd spend some time at the pool while we waited to be called for a massage. If we didn't want a massage, that was all right, too. Nobody in this group, however, was going to pass it up.

Lou left us alone, and Xaviera and I changed from being completely clothed to being completely nude.

"Where are the towels we're supposed to get?" Xaviera wondered.

"I guess we get them on the way out," I said. And that's the way it worked. As we left the undressing room, a girl attendant handed us large towels to wear, and we wrapped ourselves in them. Just then Lou showed up, also in a towel, and took us to the main pool. It was an Olympic-size affair, with a very handsome bar on one side.

I was surprised to see everyone standing around casually nude. Xaviera, rapidly getting into the spirit of things, dropped her own towel and pulled mine off as well.

"Come on, let's swim," she said, and we dove into the pool. We swam back and forth a few times, stopping to catch our breath and to talk to the others in the pool. Here we were in the middle of New York City without a stitch of clothing on, chatting as though we were at a cocktail party. I wondered how many of the folks passing by on the street had the wildest notion about what was happening in this elegant building.

When Xaviera and I had had enough of the pool, we climbed out and dried off. We didn't put the towels back on. Things were too relaxed to get uptight about towels. We walked over to a couple of beach chairs and plunked ourselves down. Xaviera wanted her usual orange juice, so I got up and went to the bar.

"You know something," I said when I returned to Xaviera with our drinks, "you couldn't use money if you wanted to. No pockets."

We both laughed, and I was glad we'd come. I felt very relaxed and was enjoying Xaviera's observations of nearly every person in the room.

She admired several cocks and one particularly nice ass. I thought the ass came with some nice breasts too, and we had a good laugh. It went on like that until our names were called for a massage. Xaviera had a good sense of humor, and we had a laugh on nearly everyone in the room.

"Massage, anyone?" I said, getting up.

"No fucking around in there, you hear," she said waving a finger at me like a schoolteacher. I didn't bother to answer her. I had read too many things about massage parlors to make any promises.

An attendant led me into a nice-sized room with a large table and introduced me to my masseuse, a honey-blonde in her early twenties. She looked extremely healthy and had a moonshaped face and very large blue eyes. Her pouty little mouth made her appear much younger, but their was nothing immature about what filled her polka dot bikini.

"Good evening, sir," she greeted me. "My name is Linda." Her voice was very high and reminded me of the cartoon character Betty Boop. From now on that's what I'll call her.

Betty Boop indicated that I was to get on the table, stomach down, and she proceeded to give me a fairly decent massage, rubbing the oil into the skin around my neck, shoulders, and back. Wiping off the oil that hadn't been absorbed, she gave me a cooling alcohol rub. Her hands weren't very strong, but it felt relaxing just the same.

It seems Betty Boop, like half a million pretty New York women was an actress. She wasn't much for conversation, and this was about the only information she would volunteer.

Finished with my back, I turned over, and my front got the same treatment. To my surprise I didn't even get hard.

Just then, as my skin was cooling from the alcohol rub, Betty Boop said, as though she was ordering a frankfurter at Nedick's, "Now, sir, would you like your penis massaged as well?"

Aha, at last, here comes the interesting part. "Well what exactly do you have in mind?"

"I could rub your penis for you, sir ... I'm sure it would feel good."

"You mean you would use your hand to make me feel good?"

"That's right, sir, I would use my hand."

"Look, Linda, don't you think you could use something else?"

"What precisely did you have in mind, sir?"

"What I had in mind is precisely what is beneath your bikini bottoms. It would feel great over my penis."

"Oh, you mean my cunt!" she replied without blinking an eye.

"Yes, as a matter of fact, I would like them to get together for a little fun."

"Well even though that sounds lovely, sir, I'm sorry but I can't do that."

"Is it against the rules?"

"No, it's not against the rules. It's just I promised my boyfriend I wouldn't screw any of the customers."

I can't say I wasn't disappointed, but the thought of a hand-job was leaving me cold. I'd just as soon get up and leave than put up with that.

Right out of the blue, Betty Boop comes up with a great alternative. "Well, sir, I could blow you instead."

"That will be just fine, but what about your boyfriend?"

"He'll never know. I use mouthwash."

She poured a little oil into her hand and massaged my penis to readiness.

"I won't fellate more than seven or eight men during the course of a day, and the tips are good."

Oh, so now she wasn't blowing me after all ... she was going to fellate me. Her head was bobbing up and down at a fantastic speed.

I'll say this for Betty Boop, if she didn't take lessons from Miss Lovelace herself, she was born with an amazing talent. She got a fantastic amount of penis in her mouth.

I was going to come in about two seconds, so I tried to signal her to slow down. If anything she started going up and down faster. Her spinal cord had to be made out of elastic. I couldn't have held back if I wanted to. Just as her mouth went down almost to the base of my penis, I exploded a small gusher of jism inside her mouth. She kept her mouth all the way down while I kept coming, and only when the spasms had stopped did she slowly come up for air. Then down once more, and back up again to clean me off.

With a big smile she said, "Well, sir, I certainly hope you enjoyed that."

"It was very, very good, Linda." I replied. I was pretty amazed by the whole thing, to be honest. "Where did you learn to ... ah ... take so much penis in your mouth?"

"My boyfriend taught me," she giggled, and her face turned crimson. "I wasn't supposed to tell anyone that."

"That's okay. You're secret is safe with me. Give your boyfriend my congratulations for a job well done." Sitting up I asked, "By the way, is he an actor?"

"No, he's an apprentice plumber."

I had to try my hardest to hold back the laughter.

When I got back to the pool, Xaviera was talking to a few people. She waved me over, and I sat down.

"How did it go?"

"Swimmingly," I responded giving her a big wink. Feeling pretty hungry after my session, I suggested to Xaviera and Lou that we leave to get a bite to eat. They agreed, and we went into the locker room to change.

While we collected our clothes, I asked Xaviera if she wanted to bring a tip to her masseuse. When she said no, I was surprised.

"What's the matter? Wasn't she any good?"

"No. It's not that, Larry. It's just that I'm the one who should get the tip."

"Do you mean what I think you mean?"

"I mean I already took care of her. She should

pay me for the fastest flick in town." She stuck out her tongue in a naughty way, lest I miss her meaning.

"How was she?" I asked, expecting the worst.

"Delicious. Larry, really, they shouldn't allow such beautiful girls to give massages. I was oozing as soon as my eyes caught sight of her. The other thing that seems so silly is those polka dot bikinis. My masseuse had red hair and I knew her cunt would be a beauty. I couldn't resist pulling the strings on her suit when she had me on the table."

"She didn't seem to mind, because when I slid my finger inside her, she was already wet. After a few minutes her cunt was so close to my face I couldn't resist. I sucked her clit and tongued her until she came. I could have eaten her for hours, she was a beauty."

"I hope you have some appetite left for dinner," I said a little sarcastically.

"I'm famished. How about you?"

"Oh, I've worked up a little appetite." I said looking as mysterious about it as I could.

We ate Chinese food that night.

You know what they say about Chinese food.

So later on that night, the two of us had a little snack. I ate Dutch, and Xaviera ate American.

Intermission in Atlantic City

In case you think that my life is nothing but sex-sex-sex, I'll tell you about a weekend Vanessa and I spent in Atlantic City. To avoid traffic, I decided it would be a good idea to fly there. However, my own plane was tied up with a leaky gas tank, so I called my pal, Stanley. He owns his own plane, too, and we had flown many places together in the past. I wondered if he and his girlfriend would like to join us for the weekend—and fly down in his plane. I must explain, Stanley is one of my flyboy buddies. We kiddingly call ourselves "the flying crew" or "the flyguys." We've both been into flying for about 15 years now, and it's like one happy family.

Stanley thought Atlantic City would be a very good idea, so I made the necessary arrangements at Deauville Hotel. His companion would be Jena, a most attractive lady who fled Cuba to escape the Castro regime and is now living in New York City with her two children. She evidently came from a very wealthy family, because when the four of us were in Key Biscayne about a month earlier, we bumped into several members of her family who live there. You do not live in Key Biscayne unless you are very well-to-do.

Stanley is a good instrument pilot who owns the same type of plane I do—a Piper Aztec. It's a small plane but seats six passengers fairly comfortably. I sat next to Stanley as co-pilot, with Jena and Vanessa sitting behind us. Normally it takes about 30 or 35 minutes to fly to Bader Field in Atlantic City from JFK Airport, where our planes are based.

When the rest of the "Flyboys" heard we were going to Atlantic City, they all wanted to join us, especially Mike, Frank, and Del. I explained that it was impossible to get additional reservations at the hotel. They insisted that, before leaving, we at least have dinner with them at some restaurant near the airport. It took a lot of explaining to get them to let us go. We had to promise that it was OK for them to fly down the next day and join us in Atlantic City.

As I mentioned, we Flyboys have been flying to various places for almost fifteen years. We meet on Fridays, Saturdays, or Sundays and take as many planes as we need, depending on the number of guests we have, and we fly somewhere for lunch or dinner. We might go to Martha's Vineyard, Boston, Cape May, or Montreal. The trip to Montreal, for instance, would take about two hours. We would arrive about 12:00, have lunch, walk around and then return to New York about 6:00 that same evening. We have been doing this for so many years, depending on good flying weather, that most of the top restaurateurs within a two-hour flying radius of New York City know us by name. When we appear, we're warmly greeted by proprietors and maitre d's, which insures immediate seating. We're generous tippers, hearty eaters, and jovial patrons. These trips are one of our greatest enjoyments.

Well, we took off for Atlantic City, and weren't airborne for more than five or ten minutes when we ran into rain. The airport weather bureau had assured us that it was pretty clear up above, and that there was no reason to run into this type of weather at an altitude of 3,000 feet. There was nothing to worry about because we were in radar contact with JFK, and they said that the rain would end shortly. As we got a little farther south, about 10 or 12 miles from New York, we started to hit really heavy rain and turbulence. We radioed radar control at JFK to hand us off to McGuire Air Force Base for further vectoring. McGuire informed us that if we were to continue south, we would run into a very bad thunder shower. They advised us to make a right-hand turn and head inland to escape the storm. We didn't see any further rain, thunder showers, or lightning, but it took us almost an hour and a quarter to get to our destination.

I must also say it was a very rough ride, and I'm sure both Jena and Vanessa would have preferred a bumper to bumper automobile trip. They both looked a little green. But they were good sports and didn't complain. At the airport we took a limousine to the hotel.

After we had rested for a while—that's all, honest—the four of us went to the Knife and Fork, a lovely restaurant where we had a wonderful seafood dinner. Then we walked on the boardwalk for an hour or so and returned to the hotel and went beddy-bye. The fresh salt air has a faculty for making one very, very tired. Although Vanessa and I had every intention of making violent love, we both soon realized that the flying escapade had exhausted us ... and we just fell asleep.

The next morning was bright and sunny. What a beautiful way to start a perfect weekend! Before getting dressed, we discovered that one of the twin beds in our room had a faulty vibrator system. The damned thing didn't stop vibrating unless you detached the electrical cord. You didn't have to put a quarter in—it worked continuously. "That's OK," said Vanessa, "I love it. I might marry this bed, Larry. When I turn it on, it turns me on! A mechanical lover. What a gas!" We started to make love on this vibrating machine. I was on my back and Vanessa was sitting on my cock, moving quickly up and down. The stimulating vibration of the bed, Vanessa's movements, and her saying, "I'm fucking *you* for a change, Larry. Come with me!" was entirely too much to contain.

We were ready to explode and crash inside each other like a head-on collision, when Stanley knocked on the door.

"Ready for the beach?" Stanley shouted.

"Oh shit," Vanessa whispered, "tell him to go ahead, Larry."

"I can't," I panted. "Maybe he'll just go away."

"Come on, Larry, let's have breakfast and go to the pool. The day is beautiful." Stanley insisted.

"Give me ten minutes," "I weakly replied. Vanessa was understandably frustrated.

"Larry, I can't really make it. I just can't come now." I still had my hardon and hated Stanley for the moment. "You owe me, Larry," Vanessa smiled. "We'll resume later, OK?" Our interrupted love session made us horny as hell, and we couldn't wait for later in the day when we'd resume with more passion than ever. What a head start!

A day at the pool, lunch, and a two-mile walk on the boardwalk made us tired, but we felt relaxed and happy. Still, we were looking forward to the fuck we started but hadn't finished.

The sun can be enervating, especially to people like Stanley and Jena, who are not devout sunbathers like Vanessa and me. Stanley couldn't wait to take a nap before dinner, and he and Jena planned a long siesta, as they were both utterly exhausted. They left for the hotel while Vanessa and I continued our stroll, with a little shopping on the way. We walked back to the hotel, intending to take the elevator to our room for some privacy. But Stanley came running up to us in the lobby and announced that the "Air Force from New York" had arrived. I took one look at the expression on Stanley's face, and rather than burst out laughing, I told him that we were going to sneak up to our room and that he should take over.

"No way!" said Stanley. "Everybody's in the bar. Come in and join us. Please help me out!" With that pathetic look on his face, I knew I couldn't leave him at that moment. Vanessa and I followed Stanley into the bar and there we saw all of the boys sitting with their girlfriends at a big round table.

Vanessa, in her Italian manner, went over to all the guys and kissed them on the cheek. We sat down with them and ordered vodka and tonic. I told the guys that since they hadn't called up earlier in the day, we had already gone for lunch to a terrific seafood place in the neighborhood and we weren't eager for an early dinner. It didn't seem to move them, and I realized that they had no intention of leaving—they were going to have dinner with us, no matter what. We wouldn't be hungry until at least 9:00 or 10:00, and it was only 6:00. Truthfully, looking at Vanessa, I knew she wanted to be alone with me. And I felt the same. What to do with the guys??? Good question, but there was no answer. We finally did manage to escape. Vanessa asked everyone to excuse the two of us, explaining that we had to go back to the boardwalk to buy some souvenirs. We told everyone we would return shortly.

Naturally, our scheme was to get back to our room without letting anyone know. We were so horny, our crotches felt stickier than all the salt water taffy in Atlantic City. But how were we going to make our scheme work? As we got ready to sneak up to our room, I became a little alarmed. Suppose Stanley and the crew decided to go up to his room, which was right next to ours? When we got off the elevator, they would see us. I decided to find out for sure and walked back to a phone booth on the boardwalk, where I called Stanley's room. Yes, he answered the phone. Yes, the whole crowd was in his room.

Stanley begged for aid, accused us of being in our room and calling from there. I said, "Look out of your terrace window so you can see us." He did, and we waved to him. Behind him, all the other people came out on the terrace, too, and waved at us in the Italian fashion—the cocking of the arm meaning "fuck you," and a few other choice ways of expressing themselves. We convinced Stanley that we'd be back soon and that we were still shopping. The master plan of attack—to sneak back behind enemy lines. We walked back upstairs, afraid to take the elevator. Luckily, we were only on the fourth floor! We opened the stairwell door and sneaked past Stanley's room to ours. We opened our door and tiptoed in. Remember, the walls are like paper in most hotels so we had to be extra cautious and quiet. We heard the noise coming from their room, but it didn't bother us at all. The sounds completely disappeared as we made love—and fell asleep in one another's arms.

It must have been an hour or so later that we picked up the phone to call Stanley. "We're ready," I shouted into the receiver. "We just got back! Let's get dressed and go to dinner."

"How soon will you be ready," Stanley wearily asked.

"I told him about fifteen minutes.

"OK, give me twenty, and we'll meet you in the lobby." Then as an afterthought, Stanley whispered into the phone, "I have the keys to the plane, you bastard. Remember that!"

Twenty minutes later, the funniest scene took place. Here came the "Air Force" boys, very much alive and ready to go, with Stanley literally dragging his ass, followed by Jena who, I would say, had aged ten years in the last hour. As Stanley walked up to me, I saw he would have killed me if given the chance. "Larry, you bastard, I should just leave you here to walk to New York.

Some friend you are. I don't know how you managed to fuck me, but you did. I haven't gotten ten minutes of sleep today, and you, you bastard, look completely refreshed and ready to go. I should have let them in your room. Six people in my room, all talking, laughing, and having a great time—Larry believe me, I'm fighting to keep my eyelids from closing."

I burst out laughing like you wouldn't believe. I didn't explain; I couldn't have anyway. I was laughing too hard.

We took a taxi four or five blocks to Jerry Trench's Neptune Inn where they gave us a table upstairs for ten people. We had a wonderful time. I wasn't too sure about Stanley though. Once or twice during the course of the meal, Jena had to kick him under the table because he was losing his fight with fatigue. We had a fabulous lobster dinner and most of the others had flounder stuffed with crab meat. We ate like kings.

After dinner, while we were standing in front of the restaurant, I came up with a wonderful idea. "Let's go dancing," I said, and Stanley almost passed out. Jena grabbed him and held him upright. I figured the rest of the crowd would opt for going back to Bader Field for the return flight to New York, and they did. It was almost 11:30, and by the time they'd arrive at JFK and drive home, it would be in the early morning hours. The flight to New York from Atlantic City is only about 35 minutes, but sometimes the late-night air traffic can be surprisingly heavy. Some of the boys lived in Brooklyn and it could take them almost an hour to get home from the airport.

After saying goodbye to the guys and their dates, I got Stanley back to the hotel by way of the boardwalk. I never laughed so much in my life, because he knew something had gone on that day, but there was no way I was about to admit it. Sorry, Stanley, now you know.

Even as I write this little episode, I am laughing to myself, because it was one of the funniest things that has happened to me in a long, long time. I must say that our little "Air Force" is a wonderful bunch of guys. While I've never had to ask for their help, I'm sure they would stand behind me 100 percent if the time ever arose.

I saw Mike, Frank, and Del a couple of days later in the city. They cross-examined me for about five minutes to find out what was really going on in Atlantic City. They didn't suspect that I had gone back to my room. But I think they did suspect we had been invited to some celebrity-type party, and that we had left them out. They thought that Stanley's being tired was just a put-on, and that he was trying to get rid of them earlier in the evening. They told me that when Stanley said he wanted to go up to his room alone, that they should wait in the bar until Vanessa and I returned, and that they ought to tag along with him upstairs, so he couldn't slip out and join me and Vanessa at this nonexistent party.

Regardless, it's a lot of fun to be able to jump in a plane, move all around the New York area in minutes instead of hours. You save an awful lot of sleep that way, and have more time to make a lot of additional love—not war.

Say, this chapter was supposed to be sort of an intermission, to show that I really do something else besides balling. Oh, well, you know how it is once you get into a habit.

Acapulco, and the Girls Around the Pool

Here I am in Acapulco. Only this time I'm here alone. Xaviera is in Canada, and I'm a little lonely. I don't know when she'll be back in the States.

I've met some really nice people down here, so it's made my vacation more exciting.

This morning I was sitting on a lounge, with my eyes closed, soaking up the sun. When I opened my eyes, there were two girls standing at my feet with a copy of my book, looking at my pictures and back to me.

A few minutes later things got exciting. They sat down on the chaise next to me, and we started talking. They began telling me how the night before they'd had a run-in with a guy who wanted to sell them two hammocks "for nothing." For nothing, hell. They could have the two hammocks if they would go to this room. We began talking about the proper way to ask a girl to go to bed with a guy.

I turned to them and said nonchalantly, "I don't blame him really. I'd love to take you to bed." Before I knew what was happening, one of the girls said with a smile, "One of us, or both?" I smiled back and said, "Both."

"We're not staying at this hotel. We're staying with two other roommates across the street. Can we go to your room?"

These girls were about twenty years old. They were going to the University of Wisconsin and had come here for a one-week vacation. Penny had black hair down to her waist, which was very narrow. She had a cute pointed nose and nice-sized breasts. Her thighs were strong and tapered down to very beautiful legs.

Francine was a blonde. Her hair was cut in a shag, similar to the cut Jane Fonda is known for. She also had lovely breasts, a nice-sized waist, and gorgeous legs. Penny was about four shades darker than Francine.

Not knowing whether or not they were serious, I got up, took the key from my waistband, and said to them, "Shall we go?" They both jumped up and followed me. We got in the elevator with a half a dozen other people, and got off on the sixth floor. Putting an arm around each of them, I led them toward my room. We walked to my door, and I took out the key. Then while looking both of them in the eye, I turned the key in the lock and opened the door. I let both of them walk past me into the room. They were both wearing very abbreviated bikinis. I closed the door behind me and locked it. Then before anyone could feel uncomfortable, I put an arm around each of the girls, pulled their bodies to me, and planted a kiss on each of their ears. We walked through the little foyer where the closets and bathroom were and came into the fairly large bedroom, which had a king-size bed.

I stopped the two girls and said, "Look, let's make like we're in St. Tropez." Very gently, I took off their suit, tops. I then could see that there was a little bit of embarrassment between the two of them. I quickly went to my homemade bar and poured a couple of cold drinks. The tensions seemed to lessen as they settled on either side of my bed, nursing their drinks. I sat between them. Then I fell to my back, and with my hand on each one of their necks, I pulled them down beside me. The drinks ended up on the floor.

The girls were sort of placid, lying there waiting for me to do something. I didn't disappoint them. I took each of their hands and placed them close to my body. They knew what I wanted and with their hands touching each other, they opened the string on my bikini, and slid it off. Their hands were wrapped around my cock, and fondling my balls. They were in a position that they could watch what was happening. My hands were massaging their breasts. After a few seconds, I ran my hands down to their bikinis, and slid them underneath. I took my middle finger and started to rub their assholes, and as if magnetized, the girls stiffened. It was then that I bent down and pushed their hands away from my cock. Very unceremoniously, I pulled their bikini bottoms off. I was a little surprised to see they had cut their cunt hairs. I jumped back on the bed. I gently pushed Penny's head toward my throbbing cock, while with my other hand, I brought Francine's head up to mine and started to kiss her. Penny at first didn't seem to know what to do, but she caught on real fast. With open mouth she started to receive my throbbing prick. After a few minutes, feeling I was going to come, I pushed her head away, and, raising my body up a little higher, I pushed her head back so that her mouth was opposite my balls. She really knew what she was doing, as she started to nibble and kiss and tongue them, which started to drive me crazy. In the meantime, I had been playing with Francine's mouth and with my other hand playing with the cheeks of her ass. I leaned down as far as I could, and my middle finger reached her cunt. I quickly slid it in. She was very wet. I took out my finger and placed it by her asshole, and with very little pressure I was inside. About that time Francine decided to take her right hand and put it down at Penny's head. With Penny licking and Francine touching, there was nothing left to do but come all over myself. I pulled the girls back into my arms with their heads on my shoulders, and we rested this way. Finally I asked Penny to get up and get a warm wet washcloth to clean Francine and me. My prick still maintained a stiff, hard appearance, and I could feel I was getting ready for the second time around.

Penny came back with a warm washcloth and wiped my stomach, cock, and balls. The girls were no longer embarrassed to be naked in front of each other. I had become the teacher, and they both seemed eager to continue. It was the innocence they had about it all that increased my passion and nearly drove me crazy. After a few minutes of their horsing around, I knew I would come again. I pushed them both away and started a conversation about sex in general. All the time my eyes were glued to their bodies. Their eyes were glued to my face, awaiting my suggestions. We talked and kidded around, and then I got the two of them to try eating each other. Seeing that they completely disliked that game, I stopped them. I had thought it would be fun, but they weren't into it at all. If I had insisted they continue, I think they would have gotten up and walked out.

It was then that I asked, "Who should I fuck and how?" It was like two kids choosing up sides.

They played a game with their fingers—odds and evens. Francine won, and I got her. With Penny still on the bed, I climbed on top of Francine and started to fuck her. I could see that Penny was a little embarrassed sitting there watching this going on. She got up and moved to the bottom of the bed so that Francine would not see her.

Once again, fearing I might be coming, I moved Francine's legs together, and moving my two legs on the outside of hers, I moved until I was in a sitting position with my prick in her cunt. I was actually sitting on her legs and looking down at her. With my hands I started to massage her breasts. I was in her, but there was no movement. I could look at her and play with her breasts. Doing this for about four minutes, I felt a hand starting to rub my ass. I took my legs and moved them back to between Francine's legs. Francine was coming. Her body kept vibrating. She moaned, just short of screaming. I almost came right then, but managed to fight it for another few minutes. I put Francine's legs over my shoulders and came in her after a few more violent thrusts. This was crazy—twice in ten minutes.

Later, having washed myself, three naked people sat down to drink. I knew that Penny was waiting patiently for me to have another erection. As we drank, Penny took an ice cube out of her soda glass and placed it next to my shrunken cock. With the two of them working on me, it wasn't long before I had an erection again. This time it was Penny's choice. She threw me on my back and got on top of me. Francine didn't seem to be embarrassed, and sat right next to me while Penny went up and down, riding my cock. Suddenly someone's cunt was over my mouth. Francine had gotten the idea and had straddled my mouth, putting her exposed clitoris over my mouth. I started to lick and tongue this little raised hard piece of flesh.

Like a director, I pushed myself up and pushed everybody off and created what is called a daisy chain. I let Francine lie on her back with her legs open, and I got in between her so that I would easily be able to lie on my shoulder and lick her clitoris while Penny was able to put her body under mine so that I could fuck her. Nothing could stop me from having this third come. When I was just about to, Penny jumped off and created a true daisy chain by putting my cock in her mouth. With me eating Francine, Penny started to eat me. When I heard Francine start to come with gasping noises, it aroused me to such a point that I got ready to come. I had not realized that Penny was being eaten by Francine. What I couldn't get the two of them to do earlier, they were doing by natural instinct now. Francine was eating Penny while Penny was eating me and I was eating Francine. As I came, so did the two girls.

We were in the room for another half-hour or

so, and then got ready to go downstairs. The girls had taken pictures with me, so I gave them one of my business cards and asked them to please send me a copy of the pictures.

Although they seemed shy when they first came to my room, it was a completely different story with the pictures. Francine insisted one picture be taken with me standing behind her. She, of course, was completely naked.

That evening and the next day, I looked for my two young lovers, but I really knew in in my heart I would not find them. They had accomplished their mission. I wondered if they would look me up in New York.

The next night I went to Armando's LeClub and did a little dancing. I walked into the lobby of a hotel Xaviera and I stayed in and picked up a sheet of paper and an envelope in order to write her a letter. I thought she'd get a kick out of seeing the stationery. Then I went next door to Boccacino's where I did a little more dancing and spent some time talking to Pepe who managed this place.

The weather in Acapulco was magnificent. The pools had five girls to every guy. I had come down to get a suntan, to do a little bit of work on the book, and mostly to relax.

One day I went down to the pool early in the morning and selected the same chair I'd had the day before. I took my black bag, laid it on top of the towel, and went to have breakfast. Coming back after eating, I noticed a lot of people were sitting around my chair.

After a couple of uneasy moments, a couple of elderly women came over to ask me if I really was the Silver Fox. When I said yes, the fun began. From 10 in the morning until 3 in the afternoon, I had nothing but admiring people asking me all types of questions about all sorts of things. This was a real up for me. It was the first time that instead of following behind Xaviera's skirt, I was attracting people by myself because I was Larry, the Silver Fox.

I went to my room and napped until a little after nine o'clock. I had dinner alone that night and felt a little sorry for myself.

On my last full day in Acapulco, I was having a ball at the pool. I asked four girls who were friendly if they'd care to join me at about 6 o'clock for a night on the town.

Lizabeth was twenty-six, had blond hair, and a bosom right out of a girlie magazine. Lily was twenty-seven, had dark hair, and also had large, globular breasts. Joann was twenty, tall and lanky, with very small breasts. Marilyn was about twenty-nine, blue-eyed and also pretty lanky. They agreed, and we met at the Villa Vera for banana daiquiris. We lounged there until about 7, when I took them to Pierre Marques for dinner. I had reserved a taxi for the entire evening. On the way to Pierre Marques, I had the driver make a fifteen-minute detour past Puerto

Marquez, a little ancient fishing village where a couple of Tarzan pictures had been filmed. We drove through. The shoreline is edged with little shacks.

On to the Pierre Marques Hotel for dinner.

I asked the driver to come back in two hours. As we walked into the restaurant, the maitre d' recognized me immediately and gave us a very good table right near the music. We had a great dinner. Around 10:30 our taxi driver picked us up, and we drove to La Huerta. As we pulled into the courtyard, I thought the place was closed because the band and the people were not in the center area. Instead they had opened up a new, much more lavish area where the girls mingled with the guests.

The taxi driver insisted on taking us to La Quebrada. This is where the dive is performed at night. The dive was from a rock shelf 136 feet above the water. The diver went before his little altar and prayed. Newspapers then were set on fire all around the rocks below so the diver and the audience would have a clear view of the water.

In thirty seconds the whole thing was over. He took a majestic dive into the water, and everyone applauded him as he came back up the sides of the rocks. We watched it from a nightclub in the Mirador Hotel. It was so crowded they took us to an empty floor below and we had a much better view. Around the outside of the hotel overlooking these rocks, there must have been about 5,000 other people congregated to watch. There is a narrow cove the diver jumps into, and you get the illusion he's jumping off the Empire State Building. The walls seem to close in on him.

After hitting a few more nightclubs, I surprised everybody by dropping the girls off at the hotel. I think they were a little surprised that I didn't try to take at least one of them to my room. I truly enjoyed the evening, and I was not looking for a bed partner that night.

Or so I thought. A few minutes later there was a quiet knock at the door. I was in the tub, so I just called out that whoever was there should come in. Luckily I hadn't remembered to lock the door.

When the door was closed and no one had announced herself, I got a little nervous. In a few minutes, however, when a naked Lizabeth entered the bathroom, I relaxed. My cock didn't though. It stiffened as I stared at Lizabeth's amazing breasts.

Except for her large breasts, she was quite small. I learned this as she stepped in the tub and sat right on my stiff cock. It slipped effortlessly into her cunt. She rode me for a while and eased herself off, turned and held my cock so the head was out of the water. She then sucked me till I came. We relaxed for a while, toweled off, and went to bed.

The next day was my last in the sun of Acapulco, as that night I had to catch a plane back to good old JFK. As the plane took off and I looked back over the town in the distance, I wondered how long it would be before I returned again to wonderful Acapulco—and would I be alone?

To London, by Hook or by Crook

In the middle of October 1972, I was sitting in Xaviera's hotel room in Canada when she got a telephone call from a very good friend of hers in London—Baron Gusta calling. Xaviera immediately ran to the phone and started speaking with Gusta. She motioned me to the telephone and holding her hand over the receiver said, "Last Sunday there was a big exposé about my still conducting a house in London."

I got scared. Here we were in Canada, which has close ties with London, and Xaviera needed to stay out of the public eye, and out of trouble. Exactly what we didn't need was this type of publicity.

After speaking briefly with Gusta, she hung up. Grabbing Xaviera by the arm, I threw her on the couch. "What the hell is this all about?" You just left London three days ago, and there's news about your running a house. Before I read it myself, for God's sake, tell me what happened!"

As a matter of fact, about four days before Xaviera left London to come to Canada, I had found out that she had been swinging for money in London. A friend had called me to say that Xaviera had a very, shall we say, eccentric businessman to whom she was sending girls, and that she herself was in his company almost every evening on a sort of play-for-pay thing. I had called Xaviera to tell her to cut it out, and to remind her that she had only a few more days to be in London, and if she had to wear nun's clothing, she should wear it. There was to be no horsing around whatsoever. I explained once again the importance of London being her home, and reminded her there was too much at stake for her to fuck around.

Now, in Canada, she told me there was little truth in the story, but I should get a copy of the newspaper article. A local hotel carried the weekly paper that had run the story. I wasted no time getting there, bought the last two papers they had, and raced back to a very upset Xaviera.

Handing her the newspaper, I showed her a foot-high picture of herself in a tiger print bra and panties, captioned by the following big, black headline: "The Madame Who Shocked Lord Porn." Then in very bold print underneath, "The

Happy Hooker Is At It Again." The copy, which continued on page 3, read, "The Happy Hooker and the One Thousand Pound Orgy."

I felt sick. I didn't know what to say. But as sick as I was, Xaviera looked a little sicker. I asked her if she had ever met the reporter who had written the article. I started to read the main parts of the story. It stated that green-eyed Xaviera Hollander, the notorious New York Vice Queen who said she was retiring from the game after writing her life story, *The Happy Hooker*, was in fact planning to set up a prostitution ring in London.

Before my very eyes, in stark black and white, were all the sordid details of Xaviera's London life. I was burning up as I read accounts of her thousand-pound scene with some millionaire's son. I was even more annoyed when I realized how stupid Xaviera had to be to fall for the three investigators who had moved into her building. When it came to a fuck, better still, fucking for money, there was no stopping her.

For 80 pounds and dinner she gave the investigator a striptease—which I'm sure was surpassed by none. By the time she was completely naked, she was so turned on by herself that she put on a little show. Meanwhile, this guy's not responding, so she throws all her cards on the table. Wiggling up to him and toying with her cunt, she goes for his zipper, but he pushes her away. But this time

Xaviera is so angry, she just throws him out and returns to her own devices.

On and on the story goes until I can barely breathe from all my anger. I was aghast. I didn't know what to say. I was afraid that Xaviera's wonderful dream of living in London had just blown up in her face. When the magazine she was writing for got news of this, I was sure she'd be out of a job.

I immediately went to Xaviera's desk and picked up her red book. Turning to the section titled "Money Received Last Week," I nearly screamed. It was all there, every pound, including the name of the guys and girls she had used, along with amounts for each night. New York Revisited.

After about five bewildered minutes in which I reread the article at least three times, I threw Xaviera on the couch, and, on the verge of hitting her, whispered, "Why?"

I got no answer. Unable to hold back any more, I blew up at her. I think anybody two blocks away could have heard the next three minutes of the one-sided conversation that I held with her. When I finally quieted down, she started to explain.

She told me how she had been introduced to some businessmen by a friend of hers over dinner one night. Supposedly one of them was a publisher interested in doing a foreign edition of *The*

Happy Hooker. Xaviera wouldn't miss a chance for fame and money, so she agreed.

Over dinner she found that her friend had a few other things in mind as well. It was fucking that was uppermost in his mind, and he wanted her for three or four days.

Xaviera decided on a base figure of 1,000 pounds, and any extras would be more. Little did she know what she was getting into. She tried sending some girls over, but her friend wasn't interested, he wanted her. So ... off she trotted, flattered, I'm sure.

That was her first mistake! This guy was a known sadist, but leave it to Xaviera to make the best of anything, she charged him 20 pounds extra for each spanking.

I felt sick. It's a small world. I knew who this guy was and was certain spankings were only the beginning.

I still didn't understand. "Xaviera, how the hell did the newspapers find out?"

She then told me about the three investigators who had moved into the building and how she fell for their whole scheme.

When she told me what happened, it all seemed so innocent. Poor little Xaviera fell for the big bad man and, of course, his money. I didn't believe a word she said. Supposedly they all went to dinner at about 8 o'clock one night. It was while they were having dinner that Tim had reached across the table, had taken her face very gently in his hands, and planted a kiss on her lips. "Tim, I want you to know you've just kissed the lips of the girl who has sucked a thousand cocks."

It was also over dinner that he proposed the 80-pound scene that the newspaper reported so well. In Xaviera's version, that is where it ended.

No striptease, no fuck—fat chance.

Xaviera left Canada a month later, for a vacation with me in Nassau. Then she went back to Europe, and I returned to New York. Before I left, she pleaded with me to come to Holland with her, and to London to get her clothes. She was afraid to go back there alone. Suppose she was recognized by the press. She couldn't say that the newspaper story was a joke, because undoubtedly the paper had proof, and if she admitted the story, they would throw her in jail or deport her again.

It was two months later when I went to Gusta's office to help Xaviera take all her clothing back to Holland, and I found the whip that she had bought for her eccentric businessman. She bragged that it had made her $3,000 in two days.

I broke it in half and hid it behind some packing crates in Gusta's storage room. I looked for Xaviera's diary. Listed under Monday, October 9th, was, "80 pounds, dinner with Tim, Lois, and Bob." Then I saw listed the episode with her businessman dated from October 5th to the 8th. It also showed that Susan, Liz, and Tamara had been paid by Xaviera for helping with this guy's sadistic fetish. I looked in her telephone book under the heading, "Girls—London." It was packed with names, addresses, and telephone numbers.

Had the story about London been true or had Xaviera written these entries just to impress me? OK, I'm impressed.

But do you know the funny part—Xaviera fucks not just for the money, but the thrill of doing it under everyone's nose without getting caught. It's like doing it in a plane, or in a phone booth in Times Square with everyone walking past. She'll immediately drop to the ground and give a blow job in any corner where she might be seen. It's the intrigue, the risk of getting caught that turns her on.

> There was a young girl called Xaviera,
> Who succumbed to her lover's desire.
>   She said, "It's a sin,
>   But now that it's in,
> Could you shove it a few inches higher?"

The Pimping of a Prostitute

One day not too long ago, I left the 21 Club and was standing on 52nd Street when I saw a very attractive young girl about eighteen years old walking toward me.

She was a strikingly beautiful redhead. The thing that really drew my attention to her was the big guy who was walking next to her, and, more important, the way they were walking. He had his left arm around her, sort of holding her up, and had pulled her right arm around his body and was holding that arm tight with his hand. He had his fingers entwined in her fingers. They seemed to be weaving sideways a little, as if one of the two was drunk. As they came next to me, I heard the girl say to the guy, "Please, let me go." He paid no attention and kept walking.

I started to follow them, trying to keep up with their pace. I couldn't hear the rest of the conversation, but I noticed every now and then she would try to stop, and he, with his arm around her, would pull her forward. I now walked quickly past them up toward Sixth Avenue, looking for a policeman. As luck would have it, there was not one in sight. Continuing across 52nd Street to Broadway, I noticed a policeman standing about a half block down the street. I ran up to him and asked him to follow me back to the corner, and I explained as we walked. I told him there would be a couple in the middle of the block coming toward us. I quickly gave the policeman a description of the guy and girl and explained to him what I thought was happening.

About a quarter of a block away, we both saw the couple approaching. The policeman started to walk toward them, and I crossed the street and started to walk down the other side. He finally reached them, and they stopped. I watched as this guy took his arm from around the girl, and she started to sink to the ground as if her legs were made of rubber. The policeman caught her, as she ended up sitting Indian style on the pavement. All of a sudden, the guy turned around and took off. I guess the thoughts that had been going through my mind had been correct. Evidently, this guy was up to no good.

Why I did this, and how I knew what to look for is another story.

About six or eight months before Xaviera left the United States and after her second arrest, she received a phone call from one of her customers. He had just had a girl in his apartment, a real pretty brunette, young and well built. He had met her on the street. It had cost him only $25 and he was wondering if Xaviera might be interested in this kind.

Xaviera got many of her girls through the recommendations of customers and friends. Some of them meet the girls, date them frequently, but won't support them. These guys would bring the girls to Xaviera's attention. She would interview them and use the ones she liked. After Xaviera's arrest, most of her girls were afraid to work for her, and she needed some staff desperately. She eagerly requested the girl's number, called her, and invited her to come to the apartment. Maybe she'd use her as a roommate, or perhaps a dinner date.

A dinner date had to be a very pretty girl with a good mind. She would not only go to bed with a guy, but spend the evening with him—dinner, dancing, and sometimes a show. A date wanted a girl he could talk to.

Xaviera told me of the appointment, and I decided to hang around that afternoon. About 4 o'clock, this beautiful, young kid came to the door. As I let her into the apartment, I saw she was followed by a big pimp. I knew that Xaviera would use no one, no matter how pretty she might be, if she had a pimp. A pimp only meant trouble. It put added pressure on the Madame if she cared at all for her girls. At the end of a day if there had been very little business, the Madame had to worry about sending the girl home to her pimp without money in her pocket. Possibly he would beat her up or create problems for the Madame, which, in either case, was not for Xaviera. It had always been her rule to never use a girl, no matter who she was, if she had any type of pimp or old man who dominated her.

Xaviera excused herself and left them with me. She was turned off and wanted no part of this guy. As her old man, I had to talk on her behalf.

The young girl came into the living room. I talked to the guy for about five minutes. I told him he had a beautiful girl, and in the future Xaviera would call her. He looked at the girl, who never took her eyes off him.

"Take off your clothes," he said matter-of-factly. She stood up, and without any emotion whatever, lifted her dress over her head to reveal a beautiful nude body, and sat down.

Nothing happened until I said, "OK, get dressed. She looked at her old man, and when he nodded, she dressed. We talked dollars and what the financial cut would be; he was satisfied. We shook hands and they left.

That would have been the end of the story except that a month or so later, Xaviera's roommate, Nina, stole Xaviera's black books. Trying to find her, I was told she was now living with a pimp by the name of Murray. Nina had come from Canada alone, and met Murray, who convinced her she was wasting her time with Xaviera. He told her she could make a fortune on her own, and with Xaviera's books, they could really make a bundle. So out walked Nina with the books.

When problems arose, Larry was always called —and now my problem was to find Murray. I had been told that a few blocks away from Xaviera's apartment on Second Avenue there was a cocktail lounge, which was the hangout of a lot of New York City pimps. I wanted to go and see if I could find this Murray, but I was afraid to do it alone. Xaviera had a friend who lived in the building, the same guy who protected her the night she jumped out her apartment window to the balcony below. I asked him if he would please go with me.

The two of us took off for this club the next night. When we got there, we went to the bar and had a drink. We sat there undisturbed for about twenty minutes while my friend asked around for Murray. If I found Murray, I could try to force him to return the books. Either he'd be in bandages, or, the more reasonable solution—that I could offer him some money as an incentive for returning them—would appeal to him, and Xaviera would have her books back. While we sat there, a guy walked over to me to introduce himself. It was the guy I had met with the young girl in Xaviera's apartment. I bought him a drink, and we started to talk about prostitution in general. He spread the word around that I was cool, and soon everyone at the bar seemed to relax. After all, if X was the biggest Madame in New York, I was a big man, either as her pimp or as her old man.

"How did you like the girl I brought over to X's?"

"Pretty. How is she in bed?" I asked. "How old is she? She looked so young."

"Whoa, slow down. Can't answer two questions at once. She stinks in bed. Can't seem to fake it, and she's seventeen going on twenty-eight. I have another girl you would really like. She's fifteen, but looks twenty-two, loves sex, is a nympho, and will do anything—anything."

"Sorry Xaviera didn't call you, but she has been very busy," I lied.

"Hell, I've been busy. Been making over $300 a day on both girls."

When I asked, "How did you find them so young and pretty?" this was the story he told me.

He lived in midtown on the West side, just off Eighth Avenue, and became friendly with a few steerers down in the East Village. Once in a while they would call him to tell him about a very pretty young girl who had arrived in the neighborhood. It seems these guys made the acquaintance of these young girls as they came in from out of town. They became friendly with them, dated them, and found out about their backgrounds. The most important thing they would find out was if they had run away from a happy family—one that would come looking for them if they disappeared from their homes, or who would report them missing, and possibly even hire a private detective. These guys looked for the type of girl who came from the Midwest or from poor parents—the type of girl whose parents would not come looking for her. This type of girl is the most desirable since she generally makes a good bed partner, and is a perfect candidate for a pimp's stable. A pimp will pay well for her—usually $200, but sometimes as high as $500.

After working a deal with the pimp, they arrange to have the girl at a certain place in front of a certain building at a certain time. Our friendly pimp, whom we'll call Bill, arrives in a car with a friend doing the driving. The pimp sits in the back, opens the window of the car, and calls out, "Hey, Mary." Mary walks over to the car and as she gets close, Bill opens the back door, grabs her arm, and pulls her into the car. Once in the car, he holds a nice long knife at her throat, and orders his friend to drive to his apartment. Once in the apartment, her thirty-day ordeal begins.

How many times he takes her, how many times friends take her, how many times she is beaten up, only Bill knows. The object is to completely

143

break the will of this girl. This goes on day after day. All dignity is gone. All sense of there being a fairness in this world is completely wiped out. The day is finally reached when Bill feels she will become a good money maker. He tells her he is going to bring in outside people and that they will pay money to fuck her. He also warns her to do anything the guys want, as she has been taught.

Instead of bringing in actual strangers, Bill starts bringing in his friends posing as strangers, testing to see if this girl will get one of them aside and start to plead with him to call the police. Invariably, the girl meets someone she feels that she can confide in and pleads with him to help her. The john leaves the girl, promising her whatever she has asked. He tells Bill, who goes to the girl and beats the living daylights out of her—beats her all over her body, but never touches her face.

After a while she has reached the point of no return, the point that Bill is satisfied with. From that moment on, she will do anything with anybody and never complain. To take her clothes off and expose herself in a group of people means no more to her than taking the cellophane wrapper from a lollipop.

Since she is a very attractive girl, he will not use her as a streetwalker. He will keep her in the apartment and send men in continuously. He has much more control that way. A girl like this might be good for at least a couple of years, until something happens to break their relationship.

This story will stay with me as long as I live. Seeing this girl walking down the street in the arms of this big guy, and seeing the way she was trying to get away from him, reminded me of the story and motivated me to go running for a policeman. I hope in some way I saved this girl from future problems. However, for her to allow herself to get in the position where a pimp was able to either dope her or do something to get her to go with him, I'm afraid she'll only fall prey to some other guy in a week or month from now. It's an unfortunate thing that there is no organization in New York to help destitute young kids who would like to find a job and stay straight.

After a while these kids lose all faith in humanity and sink into their own little shell, only to fall victim to the first pimp or guy who comes along with a soft voice, promising them the world.

I'm not saying all girls are forced into prostitution. Very few are. Most become prostitutes because of the security and promise of wealth from the smooth-talking pimp. They have been beaten down for such a long time that the first guy who comes along and throws them a life jacket, and gives them a little sweet talk, they grab onto for dear life. It doesn't make any difference whether they are white, black, or yellow. They're looking for someone to help them, but more important, they're looking for someone to belong to.

A big percentage of pimps treat their girls as girlfriends. They provide for their financial and sexual needs. They act as father, lover, and protector, and eliminate any need for the girl to think for herself. They make all decisions and, in most instances, the girl is very happy. She has security.

Xaviera used many girls that I always argued had a pimp. These girls had boyfriends, guys they lived with and supported. Many times Xaviera would make dates for the girls through their boyfriends. One thing you could be sure of, they were always prompt, never late. But again unrest was created between the two if the girl didn't get a lot of work.

Anyway, my search for Murray wasn't going anywhere fast. I was getting tired of listening to stories about poor girls being pushed around by their pimps. I sat around for another hour, and then left with Xaviera's friend. There would be other times to track this guy down. For a week I kept checking this place out, but nothing turned up. I decided to end my search. Xaviera was getting new girls and more clients. I had no doubt that in a short time there'd be a fat new client book and lots of new girls.

All Day, All Night in Nassau

Here I am at the Balmoral Hotel, Nassau, the Bahamas ... with Vanessa. When I first met Xaviera in Nassau, she was staying at the Balmoral Hotel. It's a very lovely hotel. The Balmoral is an old hotel with plenty of grounds, beautiful flowers, large rooms, and superb service. Every half-hour in the morning and every hour in the afternoon you can take a boat ride to the private island that's part of the hotel. Their beach is quite beautiful and secluded.

So Vanessa and I, while sunning on the beach, move to the other side of the island and enjoy each other's company.

There is a very beautiful German girl alone on the sand. She is always sunning alone, quietly. Occasionally two men come over to talk to her, and they all disappear into the uninhabited areas of the beach. I don't understand the exact relationship, but I could imagine what it was all about.

As I sit here on the chaise longue next to Vanessa, with my eyes closed, and the sun on my body, I can't help remembering Xaviera, because we met here. Being here with Vanessa makes this bit of paradise even more beautiful. Here is a girl I can be completely free with, no tensions. I can say what's on my mind, and get total faithfulness and honesty from her. I am a one-woman man and she is a one-man woman. I know as the different workers pass us they smile because we like each other. They used to smile at Xaviera because she'd had a scene with all of them at one time or another, but with Vanessa it's different. I don't have to wonder whether it is because she's been fucking them in my absence.

No, Vanessa is not like Xaviera.

When Xaviera and I were here, I couldn't understand why the telephone in our room used to ring at 12, 1, 2 o'clock in the morning. Xaviera would make me pick up the phone. Many times there was a click on the other end, but a few times a Bahamian voice would ask me to send down the chick when I was done with her.

Vanessa and I would spend long days and nights together. As I lie by the pool with my girl, both of us sun worshippers, it is wonderful to know two people can truly care for one another, can truly relate to one another, and can enjoy a vacation as a vacation should be enjoyed. Adam and Eve, when this all began, might have been forced to start the world going. My girl and I are not forced to do anything we don't want to, but I'm sure if Adam were looking down now, and Eve were beside him, there would be a couple of things they would be very jealous of while watching Vanessa and me ... they might even learn a few things.

Here in the Bahamas with Larry writing a book, I feel complete in myself. We spend sun-filled days together. Whether we're lying by the pool, or souvenir shopping in town, we feel great about being together.

During our stay, Larry and I fucked two or three times a day. If after a bath I saw Larry drying himself, soft kisses on his warm prick meant more to me than a hard fuck with the best lover in the world. I guess this is what love means, or what Larry means.

Larry means a lot to me, and no other man could take his place. I don't understand why Xaviera did so much wandering around, knowing Larry makes sex so much more beautiful for me than it had ever been with anyone else. It must have been easy for Xaviera to meet men down here. I had some very direct offers myself. I'd never tell Larry—there's simply no need to.

There were several people at our small, inti-

mate hotel. Larry and I stayed alone, away from the pack as we often do. One afternoon I was waiting for Larry on the tennis court. Since I was ready, I told Larry I would meet him downstairs. He told me it would only take him about five minutes longer.

While waiting for him, a young light-haired chap approached me on the court and said, "Where's the gray-haired gent?"

"He'll be here momentarily," I retorted, resenting his intrusion, yet trying to sound polite.

"Is he your husband?" he asked.

"Why?" I replied curiously.

"Oh, I just wondered if I'm open to ask you to join me."

"No, you're closed," I said, still not admitting my ties with Larry.

Why lie? I find deceit to a stranger or to anyone a very hard thing to swallow. Hearing my answer, the stranger left.

The reason I mention this harmless encounter is because it would have been so easy to start something with this young guy. Xaviera would have jumped right in. If my life had been devoid of love, perhaps this would have been a turn-on. If Larry wasn't complete satisfaction emotionally, spiritually, and sexually, it would have been so simple to say to this guy, "No, he's not my husband, and yes, I'll join you."

Late one day, Larry and I were sitting on the terrace of our suite at the hotel. The sun was set-ting. We'd had a great day in the sun, and I felt my usual warm, sensual self.

I leaned over the rail of the balcony, clad in gaily printed bikini panties—and a smile. Larry was directly behind me rubbing his warm cock against my ass. We talked and laughed at this sweet, sexual foreplay.

Larry then sat on a terrace chair, and I sat facing him, straddling his left leg. I manipulated my inner thigh muscles against his leg so that the vibrations reached him and sent out a "message." These thigh vibrations, coupled with my ass muscles and hardened nipples, which Larry kept fondling, sent us to our bedroom.

We stripped ourselves of our bikini underthings, and I leaned over the foot of the bed, kneeling on the floor with my upper torso folded atop the bed. Rubbing his stiff cock between the cheeks of my ass, Larry penetrated me from behind. We had a slow, rhythmic rotating fuck. Neigher one of us wanted to come right away, so we got on the bed and rolled from one end to the other. Larry was on the top fucking me, then stopping just in time. Larry eating me, me him. I rubbed my cunt along his chest, with my back to him. I mounted his cock, and did a slow, rotating grind. We just didn't know what else to do for each other—yet, we didn't want to reach the ultimate end yet.

Somehow, we reached the end of the bed and Larry was fucking me so hard, I squirmed over

*the side of the bed, my hips, waist, and shoulders
sliding onto the floor. I was upside down, on my
head, with my ass against the bed. Larry was on
the bed directly over me. Larry's prick was entering my cunt from above, which is the deepest
form of penetration. I felt every inch of him.
Larry's cock amazed me. The skin so soft. Putting it in my mouth alone drove me nuts. As he
withdrew a bit, I wrapped my hands around his
cock. My insides ached for him. Without Larry's
cock in my cunt, I never feel complete.*

*Trying to make Larry have a beautiful orgasm,
I pulled him deep inside of me and started telling
him how his big cock was filling my cunt to the
brim. He was grinding his cock deep inside me.
He pulled his prick nearly all the way out and
told me he was taking it away, while rubbing my
stiff clitoris. I was so close to an orgasm, I nearly
cried.*

*He asked me to tell him what his cock does to
me. In gasping breaths I just kept repeating,
"It's a big, big cock, and it fits perfectly inside
me." Finally, I said, "Give me your big cock all
the way in my cunt. I'm aching for you."*

*He came inside me so much, I thought his flow-
ing love fluid would never stop.*

25 Hours with Xaviera

It was early 1973 when I officially got fired. Xaviera had hired a new manager, Jay.

Even today, two years later, I fume inside when I think of him. Dear Jay with his 7 percent contract.

Xaviera never could pass up a bargain. Here was someone who would never charge her more than 7 percent. It wasn't until much later that she found out she had been hustled into signing a contract that allowed her manager to sign contracts for her, without her permission. She pleaded with me to get her out of this contract, which is another funny story. The movie she did was one of her manager's ideas.

It was nearly impossible for me to handle her business since I was so uptight about her love life, and it didn't take me long to feel a sense of relief when I lost my job.

I contacted all the people we had business dealings with to inform them to be in touch with her new manager. But Xaviera had already contacted them. This burned me a little, but reinforced my relief at being freed.

A week or so later, out of the blue, I got a call from Jay. He asked me to come to Toronto to be Xaviera's escort at a benefit being given by Liza Minnelli.

I agreed to attend if Xaviera asked me personally. And I hung up.

Fifteen minutes later she called back. "Please, Larry, come up." For over five minutes she told me how much she wanted me as her escort. Just before she hung up, she added, "And please bring the tapes with you."

All of a sudden things were perfectly clear to me. Xaviera was more interested in getting her hands on the tapes for her next book, than she was in getting her hands on me. I was holding on to them in New York, because it seemed she didn't trust Jay with them. Terrific manager— she couldn't even trust him with her work. I resigned myself to the fact that it was the tapes that were getting me invited to Canada and not Xaviera's undying love for me.

I said, "OK, see you Friday night. Please arrange for me to have my own room at the Sheraton Four Seasons Hotel. I have no intention of

154

being seduced by you. Bye now." I hung up again. Xaviera goes crazy when anyone says no to her—especially me.

Of course, I liked the idea. It would be fun for me to meet all these celebrities. Since I was already writing my book, it meant a chance to get some added material and to meet the press.

Arriving in Toronto Airport, I grabbed a taxi to take me to the Sheraton Four Seasons Hotel. This would be the first time I had ever stayed outside of Xaviera's room, and outside her bed.

Since the affair was formal, I had to wear my dress suit. I got dressed at my hotel and knew I looked pretty good. A short while later, Jay picked me up, and by his actions let me know he was running the show. We went to pick up Xaviera, who was waiting in the lobby. One thing, she was always prompt.

When we arrived at the Gardens, Jay excused himself to get our tickets. He said they would be excellent seats, since he had made special arrangements.

Xaviera and I were left standing together. She immediately asked me why I had not brought the tapes over. I told her she'd get them in the morning when it was more convenient. She turned to me and said sarcastically, "I don't want to see you in the morning. In fact, after tonight, I never want to see you again." I turned around and looked her in the eyes and said, "Goodnight, baby. I don't have to take your shit any more.

You don't even have to see me tonight," and walked out the front entrance.

While I was waiting for a taxi to pull up, I felt an arm slip around me, and a soft apology was whispered in my ear. "Larry, I'm sorry. Please come back inside."

Back inside we were met by Bob with the tickets. We were ushered into our seats, which had to be the worst seats in the house. Bigshot Bob had really made some arrangements. If we were any farther from the stage, we would have been in another country.

They later announced an intermission. I took Xaviera by the hand and told her to follow me. I walked directly to the stage area. Bob waddled after us. As we walked, people stopped her for autographs. When we got near the stage, I got through the guards, and we joined the Hollywood celebrities. They had come with Liza Minnelli to give a celebrity tennis match at the Mayfair Tennis Club in Toronto. Admission would be charged, and the money would be turned over to the Asthma Hospital. It was estimated they could raise about $50,000 from the tennis matches, and about $200,000 from Liza's concert. There were between forty and fifty celebrities, but I don't think the autograph hounds asked anyone for an autograph as consistently as they asked Xaviera for hers.

Instead of going back to our seats when the intermission was over, I arranged that we remain in the same area with the celebrities. We watched the second half of the show so close to the stage that I put my hand out and touched it.

When the show was over, everyone was asked to board a double-deck British bus for the Sutton Place Hotel.

When we got there, the party was already jumping. While I danced and talked to some of my film idols, Xaviera was hustling a Canadian film star, Steve.

Meekly she asked if I would mind dropping her off tonight. She was meeting Steve. Sure—who needs it anyway? About fifteen minutes later, we left the dining room for our hotel suites. Bob and I dropped Xaviera at Steve's then headed back to our room.

I had just fallen asleep when the phone started ringing. It was Cathy, a beautiful girl I had been introduced to at the party. She called and asked if I wanted a massage. Before I knew what I was saying, I said yes. In a little while, up came Cathy. She was wearing a lovely long dress and looked as beautiful as ever, even at 3 o'clock in the morning.

Cathy came out of the bathroom without a stitch of clothing on, and stood in the partial light of the door. She was a beauty. Tall and sleek, her body had a pink light about it. Her skin glowed. She had large breasts with rose-colored nipples, tilted upward. She was obviously aroused as I could see their stiffness. I stared at her breasts a long time. Such beauty is truly rare. I felt my cock starting to stiffen, and pushed the covers aside. I knew the sight of Junior at full mast would bring Cathy to my side. She moved closer to me, and I noticed in this new light that she'd shaved her cunt hair and there was a tattoo on the inside of her thigh. The sight of this woman was driving me wild.

As she moved her hand from behind me, I noticed she had a large vibrator, which she'd just switched on. Rubbing it along her cunt, she started a slow rotation of her hips. My cock was throbbing now, just the sight of this woman fucking this vibrator was going to make me come, but I controlled myself. I wanted to drag her to the bed, but I knew she was into her show.

Soon she started walking toward me. Without so much as a kiss on the lips, she applied the vibrator to my balls and started licking my cock. Control was getting difficult, but I wanted more fun. Shifting her legs, my tongue started exploring her cunt.

Hairless cunts are such a turn-on, and this lady's was particularly lovely. Her clit was hard like her nipples, and sliding my tongue over it, sent shudders through her body.

About two seconds later, I was sucking Cathy madly, and she stopped dead. Taking my hand, she sits me on the end of the bed and straddles me. Only putting the head of my prick inside her, she started rotating her hips in a slow sensuous motion.

This woman was such a tease, and my cock was ready to explode. Gently I grabbed her hips and guided my cock into her cunt. Immediately her muscles tightened around me. Moving her hands to my shoulders, she began a slow bounce, pushing my cock out and slowly forcing her cunt down around it again. As her movements grew more urgent, she pushed me far inside her and forced me to stand. Her legs were flung around my ass, and she tilted her body back and began fucking me madly.

This woman was insatiable. As soon as she had come once, she'd resume her frantic pumping. Her body was heaving with orgasm, and I let myself go.

The throbbing of my cock was driving her mad. She pumped harder and finally began shuddering so hard her back arched and drove her cunt firmly against my body. My cock still inside of her, we sat down. She wouldn't let me slide out of her. Finally we relaxed.

I woke up about 8 o'clock the next morning, and Cathy asked if I wanted breakfast. She was in the other room and I couldn't imagine what she'd found to eat. I thought for a moment, and as she entered the room, I realized what she'd done. A bowl of grapes and some whipped cream were on the dresser. My breakfast was not in the deep freeze.

Slowly she slid one grape, then a few more up her cunt. The whipped cream was next. She covered her cunt with it. My cock got hard and stiff.

I got up from the bed and spread whip cream on my balls and pulsating rod. Cathy helped me, then sat on the dresser and spread her legs. The cream was sweet, and her hairless cunt, made this an amazing experience. She was smooth as velvet. Now to the grapes. I forced my tongue deep inside her and circled one of the grapes, sliding it out. Cathy's hand was fondling her breasts. Her nipples needed to be touched. The other hand was stroking my head. I swallowed the first grape, then planted a full-lipped kiss on her clit, sucking it into my mouth. It was as hard as my cock, which was pleasantly cooled by the whipped cream.

I slid my tongue deep inside her for another hidden treasure. Cathy's cunt was soft and wet. My face was dripping as I extracted the last two grapes.

I rose to my feet, and Cathy's hands slid around my sensitive prick. Her fingers in the whipped cream were amazing. My big cock was itching to slide inside this lady and so I drove my whip-creamed cock into her. We both came instantly. The novelty had driven us nuts.

Cathy licked me clean and showered. By 9:00 she was gone without giving me a massage. Shucks.

At 9:30 I knocked on Xaviera's door. As I

walked in, she greeted me with, "You know, Larry, I'm really sorry I cheated on Paul last night. Steve wasn't good in bed at all."

I felt sorry for her, remembering the night I'd had with Cathy.

I brought the tapes over, and we sat down and sorted them out. She kept some for her secretary to type, and gave me the rest to bring back to New York and give the secretary who had done the other tapes. The tapes she kept she put downstairs in the vault, since she didn't trust Jay.

A little after 10 o'clock we went downstairs for breakfast. I picked up all the newspapers. Xaviera went through them all very quickly to see if her name had been mentioned at the Liza Minnelli affair. Unfortunately, she had not been mentioned.

She looked at me quizzically. "Hell, learn to play tennis," I smiled sarcastically.

During breakfast Xaviera started to tell me a crazy story about her business manager, Jay, and why she put the tapes in the safe. It seemed the day before someone had called up to say that her new business manager was an embezzler, a crook, and a thief, and that he'd been married several times. She asked me what to do. I felt like telling her to go to hell, but as I looked into her eyes, I knew I was stuck again. I told her a few people had called me to say the same thing. I hadn't wanted to say anything to her because she wouldn't have listened, and I still felt he might be

161

good for her. Furthermore, I was glad she was getting into trouble. Maybe she would appreciate me a little more. I mentioned a few of the people in Toronto who had called me. She knew them all.

"Call them, and let them tell you what a fool you are."

"I can't. They'll laugh at me."

"Go call them, damn it!" I yelled.

Excusing herself, she went to the phone and came back twenty minutes later. "I made an appointment for us to meet with Pat. He can't talk on the phone."

Cowboy Pat was a pretty honorable guy that Xaviera was very friendly with. One of the few honorable people she knew, and someone she would believe. We met him, and after we finished talking, there was little doubt in either of our minds that her business manager might be less than 100 percent honest.

I listened to her try to rationalize the whole thing. If she got her share, and he was taking $1,000 under the table for each deal, she thought everything would be fine.

I knew what had to be done. "Xaviera, let's find Jay. If it's true, I'll take care of it."

"Larry, I'm afraid."

"Xaviera, it's now or never."

"What about the movie?" she asked.

I was shocked back into reality.

"Please don't make waves. He did help me with things. I don't want my face in a bucket of glass.

Please don't do anything until the movie deal is finished. Larry, I'm scared." The fear built up in her voice as she talked. This was a very strange situation. What to do?!

After I was fired as Xaviera's manager, the movie deal I had negotiated fell through. The man we had negotiated with, Rocco, retracted his $20,000-on-sighing offer, and threatened Jay and Xaviera. If they didn't sign the new agreement, they wouldn't be walking.

Jay didn't respect any previous commitments and gave Rocco a flat no. Rocco saw stars. Xaviera was scared.

A meeting was quickly set up for the next day. By the time Xaviera's lawyer and I got there, the meeting had already taken place. It had consisted of Rocco and his friends, Xaviera, Jay, and a lawyer friend of Jay's. It lasted about fifteen minutes, and the following had been agreed upon. Xaviera would now do two movies. For the first movie she would get a $50,000 advance. She had no approval of the script, no interest in the movie, and any movie they wanted her to do, she had to do. On the second picture, Xaviera would get a big 5 percent. That broke their little hearts. Jay's lawyer, Jerry, from California, charged Xaviera $5,000 for sitting in at this meeting, a $1,000 of which he insisted be paid immediately. The other $4,000 is to be paid when Xaviera gets her advance.

Xaviera's life had been threatened by Rocco

and his men. We agreed to forestall any immediate changes with Jay until after we found out what was going to happen to the movie.

Xaviera was pleased with the results and completely erased any more frightening thoughts of Rocco or Jay from her mind.

As usual, Larry saved Xaviera and was sucked in by her all over again. A shopping trip, on Larry, of course. Dinner, on Larry, of course, and then right in front of me, she asks Paul to the press conference. I was insulted, at the very least.

All of a sudden, Jay came to my defense. He started to yell at Xaviera and asked her what sort of rat she was, letting me spend so much money on her and leading me to believe I would be spending the evening with her, then turning around and calling Paul. She knew I was aggravated. She had proved her point and all of a sudden, she was all over me. She was kissing me, she was hugging me, asking me to forgive her, and a million and one other things.

About five minutes later she turned to Bob and said, "I want to do some work. Why don't you split?"

Jay turned to me and said, "Larry, you ready to go? Let's go."

I got up to leave, and Xaviera said, "Larry, why don't you stay a few minutes? I want to discuss a couple of things with you?

Hating myself, I said, "OK, I'll stay."

Jay called back to me from the door, "Are you staying?

Jay wanted me to go down with him in the elevator. He wanted to talk to me. He was glad this little thing was settled, and we were friends. I left him at the door.

Five minutes later when I returned to Xaviera, there she was lying joyfully in the bathtub, taking a bath. After she had finished, she came out completely undressed and asked me what I was waiting for. She started to take off my clothes. Here we go again!

Ten minutes later we were lying on the bed in each other's arms, making love. Our session lasted till the phone rang almost two hours later. Goddamn switchboard. In doggy-style position, I put the phone on her spine. It had been about six weeks since we'd really made love. One thing I have to say for her, she's great in bed. The score ended up four to two. No one ever got Xaviera to come twice while in a 69 position. No one—not even poor, stupid Paul.

After we had finished, I felt like jumping out the window. I was mad at myself.

She didn't know how to apologize for getting me so angry. As a matter of fact, she didn't even have the decency to call Paul and cancel her date. I was burning mad. She used her body to make up for all the other things she couldn't give. I'd had all I could take.

Saying my goodbyes, I went back to my hotel

and packed. I wanted to be Xaviera's friend, but I couldn't be. The way she treated me at times was too degrading. What I kept forgetting was that I was as big a jerk for falling for her every time.

Encore in Acapulco

After leaving Xaviera, I didn't believe I'd ever meet anyone as wonderful as Vanessa. I didn't believe I would return to Tres Vidas to share it with someone I truly loved, but here I am with Vanessa.

This place has got to be one of the most magnificent private clubs in the world. Known as the millionaire's golf club, there are two beautiful eighteen-hole courses right on the grounds. The hotel caters to the sportsman. There are fourteen tennis courts, and if you make special arrangements in advance, they'll provide you with a caddy cart for your entire stay.

Having a choice between a villa and a suite, Vanessa and I decided on the suite. Our room is amazing. Furnished in Spanish decor, the floors are quarry tile or marble, and the ceilings have exposed beams. The dressing room alone is the same size as a bedroom in most apartments in New York City. One entire wall is mirrored, and there is a king-size bed in every room.

Our terrace is about fifty feet from the rolling ocean. In the morning we can have breakfast outdoors. Birds perch on the railing, and we can feed them crumbs. A meal becomes a total experience as you sit and watch people on horseback romp along the pure white sands. The sand is so white, it shimmers like jewels. Palm trees dot the sands and rolling hotel lawns.

There is a strange mixture of people here. Along with the many celebrities who come here because they enjoy the privacy, there are families complete with grandma and grandpa and the youngest grandchild. On any given day, you'll also find a couple of Xaviera-type girls. They are not terribly welcome by the rest of the guests and keep to themselves. As a matter of fact, when I called my friend to arrange this trip, the first thing he asked me was if I intended to bring Xaviera. If she was going with me, he suggested I try another club.

It seems that last January she was invited down for the day. After taking care of nearly everyone at the pool, she swam naked and carried on as she usually does. Since all the people had gotten what they wanted from her, at her expense, they left, and she spent the rest of the day alone. The management was not too pleased.

Anyway, that's all in the past now. I'm here with a girl I really dig, and someone who can have a day in the sun without making a spectacle of herself. This morning we're sitting by the pool, and about five people have joined us. Everyone is very interesting, so there are many stories we share with each other. Someone went to get a deck of cards, and pretty soon we were playing a game of poker. The stakes are high—matchsticks. Vanessa is enjoying the company. Although we enjoy our time alone, at other times we enjoy meeting new people and learning how they spend their time. Later on we'll have lots of time to ourselves and spend it locked in each other's arms making love in the special way we make love to each other. I get such a good feeling from knowing someone like Vanessa. It makes me extremely proud to be with her. Looking at her now in her white blouse opened to her firm breasts, and tied neatly at her waist, I can understand why people just smile at her, she's a beautiful sight.

The day passed as so many others do when you're on vacation. A few hours with our friends at the pool, some drinks at the bar, and a relaxing swim in the pool. At about 4:30 we all decided that we should have a communal dinner at the hotel. It was such a lazy day, no one felt like going into town.

At 7:00 everyone met in the main dining room.

I don't think I've ever seen so many beautiful people assembled in one place in my life, but my girl was by far the most beautiful. When we reached the table, two different men stood to pull out a chair for her. Vanessa smiled that appreciative smile she has and sat down. I sat next to her, and it was clear to everyone she was very much my girl. Later, when we danced, there was no question who she was with, no matter how many different people cut in.

As the hour grew later, Vanessa snuck up beside me and whispered that she wanted to leave. I agreed, and we said our goodbyes. I assumed we were headed back to the hotel room, but soon learned I was wrong. As I turned to walk into the elevator, Vanessa grabbed my arm.

"No, Larry. Follow me." She winked, and there was a mischievous look in her eyes.

Giving in to whatever she had up her sleeve, I followed. We were headed outside. We passed the pool and were going in the direction of a clump of palm trees on the beach. Vanessa lead me to the center of the group of trees, and I noticed we were completely hidden from anyone who might be passing by. The moonlight, however, left the area very bright, and as Vanessa discarded her dress and came into my arms, her body glistened.

"You little devil! How did you find this place?"

As she eased me out of my shirt and pants, she admitted that while I'd been resting one afternoon, she'd done a little exploring on her own.

When she found this place, she knew exactly what she wanted to save it for.

In the crystalline moonlight, we made love, and I felt like I'd never be unhappy as long as I had Vanessa by my side. I held her away from me and let the light fall on her body. She was so beautiful, and all my own. We smiled and loved as the starlight danced in our eyes.

After standing and rubbing our bodies together, we became daring and raced to the ocean. No one was around, and we let the waves roll over our nakedness, and then we stretched out on the shore. Vanessa took my cock in her mouth as waves curled around my body. She was soaking wet, and the water added to the glow of her skin. She was like a magic jewel, and I pulled her to me. We kissed long and hard, then she straddled me, and we fucked for a long time with the water lapping over us. Slowly she rode me, until her need became too great. Forcing me to a sitting position, I remained inside her, and we came, clutching each other on the sand.

Catching our breath, we sat still for a few moments, then ran into the water to cool off. A few minutes later we were back in the cluster of palm trees collecting our clothes. Sneaking one more kiss, we dressed slowly and headed back to the room. We were both exhausted.

After a quick shower, we slid beneath the sheets and fell asleep in each other's arms.

The next day was our last day in Acapulco, and

we wanted to be rested for a full day of excitement. We hadn't been on horses yet, so we were planning on rising early and taking a trot along the beach.

As I closed my eyes, I felt myself smiling with an inner contentment. All the women I'd known in my life, and this lady beats them all. Amazing what a loving person can mean.

The next morning we donned shorts and headed for the stables. Vanessa had packed a bottle of wine and a blanket. We picked up a lunch we'd ordered from the dining room and set out on two fine horses down the beach. We rode for a long time, until we found a lovely spot with some palm trees and a white beach. As I glanced up to help Vanessa down from the horse, I smiled at her beauty on the back of this animal and the knowledge that she was mine.

We lunched and, knowing there was no one around, removed our clothes and stretched out in the sun. Vanessa stood and headed for the water. I raised myself up and watched her walk down the beach. Soon she emerged, drenched. Shaking out her hair, she ran back to the blanket. The sun on my cock had added to my enjoyment of the sight of Vanessa running along the sand. I suggested we make our last day in the sun a day to remember, and Vanessa teasingly shook her wet head on me. I jumped, and she took off. I ran after her and tackled her a few feet away.

In seconds we were covered with sand, so we

headed to the water to rinse off. As soon as we were in up to our waists, Vanessa slipped her fingers around my cock. The cool water and her warm hands created an amazing sensation. I reached for her breasts, and her mouth came to mine. We kissed, long hard kisses, then I lifted her and carried her back to the blanket. Starting with her ears and neck, I licked her dry. I made sure her navel was dry and moved slowly down to her cunt. Vanessa's arms were raised over her head, and I could tell by the arch of her body that she was enjoying this tremendously.

In gasped whispers, she said, "Larry, come inside of me."

Knowing she would come soon, I slid my hard cock into her cunt. Her pelvis arched up to meet mine, and we rocked in unison to an amazing orgasm.

We spent the next few hours either in the water, or locked in a love clasp. Vanessa loved fucking in the water. Once we stood in the ocean, and I lifted her so my cock slid right into her cunt. While the waves swirled around us and the sun beat overhead, my girl went nearly wild as her body shuddered with orgasm.

When the day began to grow cooler, we mounted our horses and headed back to the hotel. We had a late-night flight to catch back to New York. After dinner, we would be leaving this paradise, but I knew a bit of paradise was coming home with me too.

I'd had a wonderful time the last time I stayed at Tres Vidas, but this time with Vanessa was like a dream. No matter what ever came between us, I knew I would always remember these last few days as some of the best days of my life. I think Vanessa feels the same way too.

Questions and Answers

Q. *Is Xaviera a wealthy woman?*

I'd say she's a millionairess—all in cash, too. I can't say what she's made in the last two years in movies, lectures, and literary pursuits, but she must have at least a million dollars, in various bank accounts throughout the world. I opened most of them for her.

Q. *Xaviera was arrested in Vancouver, Canada, for shoplifting, with all her money. What's the whole story?*

Once in Eaton's, a large department store in Toronto, a very nervous Miss Hollander came up to me and handed me her shopping bag. She said three store detectives in pink shirts were following her. "Well, don't leave me holding the bag," I said. But before we could debate whose bag we were in, we were already in the detectives' clutches. They were being very polite, smiling, and with a large gulp and a "gee whiz" sigh, I quickly emptied out the contents of her bag. It seemed there were three unpaid-for items in there, and I laid them on the nearest counter, which was men's shirts. After holding a football-type huddle, the security men were very nice about it, and to our surprise left us to our devices. However, a salesgirl came over, and I thought we might still be in for some trouble, but all she did was to ask Xaviera if she could ask her a question. Anticipating the question, I interrupted, saying, "Yes, miss, this *is* Xaviera Hollander, the famous author." This seemed to fluster her, and she walked away. My bet is that she had really wanted to ask Xaviera, "With all your money, why take three $5 cosmetic items ...?"

I grabbed Xaviera, and we headed for the bargain basement department. When we were sure we weren't being followed, we left the store. Across the street was another large store called Simpson's, and I suggested that she finish any shopping she had to do there. We wandered around quite a bit, and almost died when we realized that we'd walked into Eaton's again—and were headed toward our security friends. We turned and ran out of Eaton's budget store, laughing.

Once in Nassau we had another close scrape.

Xaviera had gone into a very smart boutique—
I'd promised to buy her her first Leonardo
creation—and Xaviera selected a lovely three-
quarter length dress that cost $180 then. While
the nice young woman who was waiting on us
went off to pack the dress, Xaviera shocked the
shit out of me by calmly taking another Leonardo
off its hanger and putting it in her large handbag. I was terrified that the saleswoman or the
store owner would notice the empty hanger, but
Xaviera simply announced that she'd wait for me
outside while I paid the bill. She grabbed her
handbag and exited, leaving me to hope that no
one would notice that there were now two empty
hangers where there had only been one. But
things went smoothly, and I paid the bill and left
the store.

I half expected someone to come running after
us, but no one did. Still, Nassau is a very small
island, and if that missing dress *was* discovered,
we wouldn't be very hard to find. In panic I
bought a newspaper, carefully placed the dress
inside it, and found a place to hide it—a crevice
between two round blocks of concrete in a wall
near the store. Later, close to twilight when the
streets were pretty quiet, we went back and got
the dress. Needless to say, we did no more shopping that day.

When we returned to the hotel to rest and get
ready for the evening, Xaviera proudly pointed
out how much money she'd *saved* me that day—

even though I had spent a bundle on her. With that kind of reasoning, I'm sure she could solve the energy crisis.

Q. *How could you allow a book to be written about yourself that would expose so many of your intimate secrets to the public?*

My answer to this question in one word, three words, or a hundred words is MONEY, MONEY, MONEY, MONEY. I was offered an awful lot of money to tell some of the fun stories of Xaviera and me that she would not necessarily want to put in print, and which Warners, the publisher of my first book, thought would make interesting reading.

Q. *Are you an exhibitionist?*

No way! I'm the guy who for over three years stood behind Xaviera—far enough behind her so that no picture was ever taken of me with her. No one even knew I existed. Oh, yes, I was her boyfriend. Some people even referred to me as the Silver Fox. But very few people ever knew my real name. Even when it came to sex, I stayed in the background. Maybe that's one reason I didn't enjoy the mass orgies, or the partousse.

When my first book came out, the only thing I was apprehensive about was having my picture on the front cover. In most instances I do not want to be recognized. As Larry, the Silver Fox, I want to go places with my girl without being hassled by the well-meaning people who would recognize me. I like the public eye. I like being a celebrity, but only when I want to be. The rest of the time I like to remain unobserved in order to lead the healthy and happy life out of the public eye that I feel I must have.

I had the opportunity to appear in *The Happy Hooker* movie. If I were ever going to be an exhibitionist, that was my chance—a chance I gladly passed up with no regrets. All that in living color. Not for me ...

Q. *What is normal sex?*

What is normal sex?—how often I've heard that question. "Normal sex" is what you and your partner enjoy doing behind closed doors. I don't care if it's hanging from the chandelier, if you both enjoy it, it's normal sex.

Q. *I've heard you refer to yourself as a shy person. Are you?*

Yes, I am. Even today, if I walk into a cocktail lounge early in an afternoon to wait for someone to meet me, and there's a very attractive lady sitting on the other side of the bar, and no one else in the place, I couldn't ask the bartender to buy her a drink, or even walk around and ask her if I could buy her one. I just can't pick up people. If I'm introduced to people or go out with people in a group, I have no problems whatsoever, but I'm shy on my own. I can't ask a girl to join me or tell her how pretty she is, which many people are able to do.

Q. *Is Xaviera happy?*

Truthfully, I think she is one of the loneliest people you could ever meet. She's always trying to make friends, mostly with the use of her body. It's really a shame. Here's a girl sitting on top of the world, yet so insecure about herself.

Q. In *My Life With Xaviera,* you speak of Frannie, the virgin. What ever happened to her?

Frannie is going for her master's degree at a well-known college in New York City, and once a week she stops up at the office to use my phone and to talk to me about some of her problems. I think she's going to be OK. She went up to see Xaviera a few times. On one occasion she talked Xaviera into tying her down and whipping her. If I could have gotten my hands on Xaviera, I think I would have busted every bone in her body. I saw some pictures of that whipping and was not too pleased with what I saw, and at that moment not very proud of Xaviera. I wonder if Xaviera was working out her jealousy over my relationship with Frannie. It was Xaviera who originally told Frannie to get in touch with me if she had any problems. Oh, well, poor X.

Q. *Do you still go out to Las Vegas?*

Oh, yes, I like the town. I go mostly in the

warm weather. Everyone knows I'm a sun worshipper. I've been on a couple of junkets with Big Julie Weintraub to the Dunes Hotel. I've also been to the Grand Hotel several times, where I've become very friendly with Jimmy Moore. Jimmy is in charge of the daytime casino there.

I like Las Vegas. It's a place I can relax in for four or five days and feel I'm completely away from business. It's almost like being up in a plane by yourself at about 8,000 feet, and knowing that you and possibly God are the only people up there, and you can relax completely, with no fears or worries.

Q. *Where do you and your girl like to go on vacation?*

Any place in the sun . . . Any place. We don't necessarily like to go to the same place all the time. We go to the Bahamas, Freeport, Nassau, Acapulco, and during the warm months to Vegas. I spend an awful lot of time in Key Biscayne, Florida. A couple of weeks ago, we went to Montego Bay in Jamaica for the first time. It's a beautiful island, but in a five-day stay we had three days of rain. The important thing is to get away from the city, and if we can go away to the sun, that's preferred. When we can't get away for a long vacation, it's up to the Concord Hotel at Kiamesha Lake in the Catskill Mountains of New York. We're not ski enthusiasts, but there's a beautiful golf course, indoor and outdoor tennis courts, indoor ice skating, and all the various amusements, including things like Simon Says, art exhibits, lectures on buying and selling stocks, and, most of all, happy people who love to dance and drink. There are five separate bands playing at all times, and if you want, you can walk from one place to the next enjoying different bands and continuous dancing. Yes, the Concord is an experience all its own. It's probably the largest hotel in the world . . . a city within a city. The dining room seats over 3,000 people at one sitting. As you enter the grounds, you're directed to one area where porters take your bags from your car and store them inside the hotel until you've checked in. Checking in is an experience too. Fortunately, Vanessa and I are well known at many of the hotels, and we can avoid some of the lines, where you could spend the better part of an hour waiting to get your key at the desk.

There are all sorts of rooms, from small singles to super double rooms, easily accommodating four people. On singles' weekends, four single strangers might share the same room. I would have to say that a day at the Concord is the most inexpensive way to take a vacation in luxury surroundings.

Q. *Are you still good friends with Xaviera? When did you see her last?*

I last saw Xaviera on her birthday, June 15. We're still good friends. We speak on the phone almost every week. About a month ago, I got furious with her. She called collect, called me a thief, and then hung up. I wouldn't accept her phone calls for about three weeks after that, until she quit horsing around.

Q. *In the back of your book you stated that you would answer anyone who would write and ask you questions. Have you done this?*

Any letter that was ever written to me has been fully answered. I enjoy hearing from people, and I keep in constant touch with people because they inevitably write back. At Christmas time I must have sent out a thousand cards. It's fun. Now people can write to me directly, to The Silver Fox, P.O. Box 143, Peck Slip Station, New York, NY 10038.

Q. *Is it true that Xaviera has quieted down, has a boyfriend, and is no longer on the prowl?*

I'll give you examples from the past six months. On her birthday she took me to her apartment to introduce me to a Bohemian girl whom she had invited to live with her for two months. Xaviera told me that she was very much in love with this girl, that this girl was her sweetheart. About that time, a very close friend of mine, Jack, the one whom Xaviera had tried to seduce in London, happened to be in Toronto and was seduced by Xaviera. No, I must say that fish do not learn how to fly. Even though I've heard she keeps three or four evenings a week for Paul, she has not changed, and she has a lot of interludes when Paul is away.

Q. *How old are you?*

I am constantly asked how old I am or how old Xaviera is. In their letters to me, many people divulge their age, almost in utter despair. Let me say that age is only numbers. We can do whatever we feel we want to do. We can enjoy our lives, have a lot of fun. We can make things happen regardless of age. From the sexual standpoint, if you consult a doctor, he will verify that not only doesn't it wear out, but the more you use it, the longer it will last. The older people get, the more they tend to abstain from sex. However, take Georgie Jessel. He enjoys a healthy sex life at his age, according to Xaviera, and so, dear readers, should you. A little advice from me to you. When you wake up in the morning, take a look at the obituary column in the newspaper. If your name isn't there, you've got it made—enjoy that day. Have a ball! And "use it or lose it." That's a medical fact.

Q. *What is the general reaction to you, the Silver Fox, when people find out who you are?*

I'll let Vanessa answer that one.

(*Vanessa*) At the pool in El San Juan in Puerto Rico, a bunch of what I'll call Jewish wiseguys are bathing in the sun, gold chains around their necks, bragging about their conquests, their gold bracelets, and anything else tagged status. They didn't know who Larry was yesterday—today they know. They've become very sheepish. They don't talk about their conquests. They eye Larry's crotch. They eye me. You can just read their minds. They seem a bit more "respectful." That's the before and after of Larry, the Silver Fox.

Q. *Did the publication of your sexual exploits bring you attention from women.*

Obviously, the answer to that is yes. Xaviera is a sex symbol throughout the world, and for me to be able to satisfy her for over three years must arouse the curiosity of many, many women.

Q. *Do you think prostitution should be legalized?*

Absolutely not! The day that prostitution is legalized in the United States is the day I will leave for foreign shores. I think that prostitution and other victimless crimes should be somewhat ignored by the police department, but they must always have the right to go in and arrest. How would you feel if you took your wife or girl to your favorite restaurant, and sitting at the bar was a beautiful young lady, and as you walked past her, she would say in a loud voice, "Hey, buddy, why don't you drop the old bag you're with and see what a good lay is like?"—and there was nothing anyone could do about it? Or maybe you decided to go with this girl to her apartment, and up there she robbed you. What would you do then? Call the police? Say you were robbed? By the time the police got there, there would be no proof of the robbery. However, if the police have the right to arrest on prostitution, even though they might not exercise that right under normal circumstances, when you report a robbery in a girl's apartment, they can go up and arrest her for prostitution. She'll think twice about robbing you. If she stands in a restaurant and abuses you or the company you're with, the police can arrest her for prostitution.

Most people will admit that most prostitutes bother no one. They're usually young girls who've come from the suburbs or from out of town to share apartments with other girls. They usually hold jobs, and unfortunately, in today's economy, they are unable to buy the clothes they need, pay the rent, and have enough money for food. So when they can meet a "dude" or a "john" once in a while for a little extra money, they'll take it. I can see nothing wrong with what they're doing.

As Xaviera so often said, the main offender of society is the streetwalker, who usually is dominated by a pimp, and can't go home unless she's had a certain number of scores or she is likely to be beaten up. She is the one who creates most of the havoc we read about in the newspapers.

Q. *Do you think gambling should be legalized?*
Heck, I thought it had been. Today, if someone

wants to place a bet, he can go to OTB, to the racetrack, to Vegas, to the islands down south. There isn't much left to be legalized.

Q. *You say you are now keeping company with a delightful woman? How does she feel about your past life with Xaviera?*

The girl I'm going with now had been previously married. I don't question her about things that happened in the past, and she doesn't question me. The past is forgotten. In the present, we just do the right thing—no horsing around on either side.

Q. *Do you miss Xaviera?*

No. It was an experience, an affair. It was a chapter of my life. Listen, no one in the entire world can say that he has had more fun than I had researching the material that appears in my books. I had a ball. I regret nothing. I still consider myself a good friend of Xaviera's as she does me. But it's over, finished. I think we're both better for it. As the expression goes, "On to bigger and better things."

Q. *What is your relationship with Xaviera since the publication of your book?*

That's an interesting question. When the book was in its infancy, and we were talking about it, Xaviera was the first one urging me to write it. When the book came out, Xaviera was very critical of its contents, but still very pleased with the story itself. But when the first printing of the book was almost a million copies, Xaviera became a little upset, and when the book went into its second printing a month later, she was frantic, furious, wild. Where does an ex-boyfriend, Larry, the Silver Fox, dare to take one square inch of the pedestal she was sitting on as a writer of *The Happy Hooker* series. She became very jealous.

Q. *Do you admit that your book is not a literary work? Do you feel there should be some censorship of its purchase?*

Again, an interesting question. Most of your affluent department stores with book sections, of the Saks Fifth Avenue type, will not have the book. If you ask the salesperson why, she'll tell you this type of store does not handle that type of book. What would happen if a minor would pick up the book in the store and start to browse through it? It would be most embarrassing. While she is talking to me, I am looking across the counter to the cash register, on which I see a copy of *The Joy of Sex*, a book that not only tells about sex, but illustrates it very graphically.

Q. *What do you think of swings, and what do you think of their participants?*

As described in Xaviera's and my books, I've been to a lot of swings. Other words for a swing are orgy, *partousse,* or, when I was a kid, I think we called them "gang bangs." The people that participate in these swings are usually a jet set group of people, people financially secure. As individuals, they're wonderful and nice people. In my travels with Xaviera all over the world, we would keep bumping into people who comprised this jet set of swingers. On December 16, 1972, Hans Gluck gave a group swing party in London to which people came from all over the world. Invitations were few; word of mouth drew the crowd.

I always thought that the women got the best of it because they could suck as many men's cocks as they wanted to, and have as many men make love to them as they felt they wanted. The cavity was always there. A woman could come as often as she wanted. For a man it was different. A man was entitled to one reaction, only every so often. But I found out that most of these master swingers were so practiced in the art of self-control, that they were able to walk around with a perpetual hard-on most of the time, satisfying all the different people they had to satisfy. The obligations included the host and hostess, and various friends. Then they could get down to serious sex.

I personally could never enjoy this type of gathering. This was not my cup of tea. Even Xaviera started to tire of the actual sexual part of it. Then we went mainly to see friends whom we hadn't seen in a long time. Sexually, Xaviera became bored. It was like ships passing in the night. Two seconds later, you forgot the face of the person you had been with. After the last few orgies we attended, Xaviera complained she couldn't even come once.

It's a strange feeling to perfume or powder your body while getting dressed, or check your underwear for attractiveness, because within three or four hours, you're going to be undressed, making love to people you'd never met before. To me, it's a little sick. Can you imagine a lineup of men waiting to fuck the hostess because they're in her house. She's giving the party, and it would be bad manners, no matter who you are, to avoid putting your prick in her cunt. At one swing, I had to do it with a charming sixty-year-old lady. I almost couldn't.

There's another thing I noticed about the "master swingers." Instead of sticking to just boy-girl relationships, it's been my experience that, given half a chance, men will go after their own kind also.

The only kind of swing that I like is when a couple, out for an evening, meets another couple or another single person, and they like each other's company. Later in the evening, instead of going separate ways, they all get together to have a little bit of a swing. This usually means four people at the most getting together for a little sex—and this can be a lot of fun. Remember, it's spontaneous.

Although swinging couples seem to be happy

on the surface, as Albert and Meis, who accompanied Xaviera for the first three or four months after her return to Europe, appeared to be, they are not always so happy deep down. Albert is in New York alone, and Meis is back in Holland. I've heard rumors of divorce.

Another thing I find distasteful—the swingers include their entire families. When a boy is twelve, fourteen, or sixteen years old, he is taught how to participate in these things, and so are the girls. I would always argue with Xaviera that if kids start heavy sex that young, what do they have to look forward to as they grow up? How can a kid of twenty-four take on a girl of eighteen or twenty and be happy with normal sex? I am square enough to believe that heterosexual love with the right person can be one step from Heaven. Overall, I think these swings are bad things.

Q. *How could you go out with a girl in the business?*

When I first met Xaviera, she really wasn't in the business yet, and to me she was a little pussycat. We enjoyed going places and doing things together. When I wasn't with her, I closed my eyes to what was going on. I rationalized that this was her job. How many girls hold nine to five jobs where the boyfriend is ever told not to call the office? Xaviera had a job also. It was from 7 P.M. through the night, Monday through Thursday.

After having an early dinner, I would drop her off at the front door. I would not call till the next afternoon. As far as her business was concerned, I minded my own business. Oh, I always wanted to get her out of the business. That was the main reason for pushing the writing of *The Happy Hooker*. But from a personal standpoint, when we were together, and if she treated me the way I wanted her to treat me, with the respect I wanted, then this was the only thing that I really was interested in.

Q. *How is Xaviera in bed?*

Any guy who is truly in love with the girl he's going with, has to find her not to be "the best," but the "very best" in bed. This was true for Xaviera and me. Sexually, nobody else could be better. We enjoyed each other fully. We made love whenever it struck our fancy. We did this any time, any place, and anywhere. When I say anywhere, I mean it literally. Be it in a ladies' room of a plane, in a phone booth, in a car, a bed, in front of people, behind people's backs—any place, any time. And, usually, just the two of us. We preferred this to any arguments since we were both insanely jealous of the other.

Q. *Why didn't you get married?*

There was a time when Xaviera wanted to marry me, and I her. But she had certain restrictions she wanted to put on our marriage, the main one being the amount of time we should spend together—or the amount of time she could cheat. She would have preferred to live with me five days a week, and to have two days to herself to go out hunting in the evening, or bring someone home to go to bed with her, while I stayed in another room. I happen to be one of those Jewish people who have funny ideas about marriage. I figured if I got married, it should be for seven days, seven nights, and seven mornings every week. I don't think I'd go crazy if I saw her cheating once in a while, but I didn't want any pre-set arrangements to be made.

Once, a few months ago in Europe, she sent me an emergency letter—"Please come over and marry me. You win. I'll do whatever you want." But at that time, I felt she was only saying it because she was so depressed that any thing seemed better than living the life she was living alone in Europe. Remember, even though it appears that you are having a ball sleeping with many partners and being seen at the best places, when the morning comes, you are alone!!!

Q. *Does Xaviera have any vices?*

If you're talking about does she smoke?—no. Does she like drugs?—no. Only recently with this friend Paul, she started to smoke pot. She won't drink any liquor. Even wine and beer she refuses to taste. She doesn't smoke cigarettes. You can't even get her to take a cup of coffee. Along these lines, she doesn't have any vices. People laughingly ask, "Well, what about sex?" All I can say is, why do people classify sex as a vice?

Q. *Will Xaviera ever be really faithful to any one person?*

My opinion is bluntly—no. Xaviera will meet what she will call a beautiful human being. Then she will stretch her imagination so that it will permit her to do what she is going to do. In other words, she'll say to herself, "Well, I'm in love with Paul today. Or, I'm not going to cheat on Clyde, but if I only give Bill a blow job, that's not really making love to him, so that's OK." This is her attitude with anyone she might be in love with at the time. So far, in all cases, these affairs she's had seem to end within two or three months, by natural means unless she starts to fight them. Then they'll last a little bit longer.

Q. *Is sex the most important thing in your life?*

To me, sex should occupy about 20 percent of a person's life, at most. I enjoy being with interesting people, having good mental relationships, going to libraries and concerts. I enjoy football, baseball, tennis, and sitting down to play a good game of cards. Sure, under normal conditions there are times when you'll get horny, and if you're with the right girl, you'll end up in bed. But if you're having a good time doing other things, it's sort of ludicrous to look at your watch and say, "My goodness, it's 11 o'clock, and we haven't even been to bed yet."

Q. *What are your views on Women's Lib?*

I never thought twice about it. When I was in the construction business, I never had to hire women as workers. As far as being around women and men all day long, I always thought that both of them were equal. It is only lately that I have heard friends make mention of the inequality in their jobs. I also have been asked to go to a few group meetings by some women who are very serious about Women's Lib. I certainly believe that equal qualifications should mean equal pay. I don't believe in men or women trying to change their appearances. I don't like the idea of men dying their hair to look more attractive, any more than I like the idea of a woman cutting her hair so short she looks like a man. I still enjoy driving up next to a car that I had been traveling behind for a few minutes, to look at an attractive long-haired woman sitting in the car. I get awfully disappointed when I discover it's a boy.

To my way of thinking, a woman can be just as intelligent as a man. As long as she can do the job adequately, I feel that she's entitled to be compensated adequately. There is no reason that two equal jobs should have two different salaries ... one for the woman and one for the man.

Q. *What is your biggest turn-off?*

With a man or a woman, there is no bigger turn-off to me than to meet someone who's well dressed and well groomed, and who smells. This is the complete and absolute turn-off. Another turn-off is to meet a girl whose clothes are not clean. Sometimes the back of the collar is black, a real turn-off to a man.

Q. *What part of a woman's body is the sexiest?*

To me, the entire body of a woman is the sexiest. But, above and beyond, to touch and taste a woman's breasts, her nipples, is the sexiest. The only other area that I think is as sexy is her lips. Just to kiss her, to relax and kiss her, something happens if she's the proper type for you to be with.

Q. *Is the Silver Fox free to date?*

Yes, for the past eighteen months, the Silver Fox has been dating. Basically, one girl. I'm the sort of guy who just can't flit from girl to girl as Xaviera could from guy to guy. I'm what they call a one-woman guy. If I'm with a girl I enjoy, then why go out looking for all different types? I'm very happy and not hard to please. I don't go looking around the corner. I'll stay on this side of the street with the one I'm with. If, after some time, we stop liking each other, then I'll look for someone else. But until that time comes, I'm happy with the girl I'm with.

Q. *What is your zodiac sign?*

I was born on June 2. That makes me a Gemini, or a twin. As a matter of fact, Xaviera is also a Gemini. She was born on June 15. There's approximately fifteen years difference between her and me, which didn't seem to hamper us one way or another. People were a little surprised that two Geminis could get along as well as we did.

Q. *What are the favorite places you like to go to eat?*

That's an unfair question, because there is no such thing as a favorite place. If I'm with the right company, there isn't any place I won't go. I can have as much fun in a Horn and Hardart's automat as I can in Brussels restaurant on East 54th Street. I can enjoy the Top of the Sheridan in Puerto Rico as much as I enjoyed some of the restaurants I went to in Paris. Make it the right company, and I can go any place for dinner and enjoy myself thoroughly.

Q. *What do you think of pornography?*

I don't particularly like pornography. I don't enjoy picking up a book and watching men and women making it on the pages, or reading all the filth that is printed. I think there should be something a little bit more subtle for our teenagers and for the public. Don't misunderstand me, to my way of thinking, *The Happy Hooker* and *Xaviera,* even though they're fun and entertaining books, I still think they're garbage, from a literary standpoint. This book I'm writing I hope will turn out to be a successful book, and will be a funny, happy book. I don't think, to quote Xaviera, that it's a "dead in bed."

In a book, on a picture, as well as in the flesh, I would rather see a little draping, a little hidden from the eye, a little left to the imagination. Then I can enjoy, to a greater extent, the article I am looking at. I've gone to some movies in midtown Manhattan. What I saw was utterly unbelievable. When I was a kid, we used to see these little 8mm pornographic movies, and I thought they were great because they were so terrible and so bad. Here, in color on screens that must be 20 by 30 feet, I watched worse acts of sex being performed in front of the public.

Q. *What type of clothes do you like to wear?*

Over ten years ago, I became aware of the changing fashions for men. I began to buy colorful shirts instead of white ones, started to wear body shirts, form-fitting suits, and all the new types of underwear. Today, I like to think my wardrobe is the greatest. My favorite is Pierre Cardin. Most of my suits, as well as the rest of my clothes, are of his design. I like the cut of his suits. I love the silk voile shirts that are so hard to get in the United States and so easy to get in places like San Tropez or London. They're see-through shirts. I like slacks without back pockets, just small side pockets. Lately I've started to like velvet suits and velvet jackets. My shorts are bikini. My socks, calf height.

Men's clothing is so colorful, why not enjoy??? While I don't like the high-heeled shoe with the multicolored appearance, possibly because I am six feet tall and I like the height I'm at now, I think they look great on many, many people. Also another reason for not wearing multicolored shoes is, I guess, I'm a little too conservative, or maybe a little too old.

Q. *What do you think of drugs?*

I classify someone who sells drugs in the same category as I classify a pimp. I would castrate all drug pushers. If they stood on a pair of stilts, they could look a snake in the eye. They are the lowest. More kids' lives have been ruined by their taking "ups" and "downs" and shooting different types of drugs. How about the families of those kids? What happens to them? I don't know too much about the legalities of possessing or using marijuana. To me, it doesn't seem that bad. I will smoke a cigarette once in a while, but I have self-control. If it's the beginning of a road that leads to hard drugs as some people in the know seem to think, then I would like to see all types of drugs completely outlawed from the face of the earth.

Q. *If you could fantasize, what would you most likely want to do for this world?*

As a kid, I wanted to be the Lone Ranger, the fastest gun on earth. I wanted to go from town to town, make things right, straighten things out. When I couldn't do it peacefully, I would go and shoot the bandit. Today, really, there's no darn difference. I'd like to straighten the world out a little bit. I'd like to have things go along so everyone could walk down the street together in one harmonious group, being friends with one another—white, black, yellow, Jewish, Buddhist, Catholic—it makes no difference. I would like to see this just one happy world, no more wars. I guess what I'm really saying is there's a need for the Lone Ranger today.

Q. *If you had a daughter, would you allow her to become a prostitute?*

Xaviera always paints a pretty picture about how much money would be made by a working girl, etc. She had to for the myth surrounding a worker. This is not true. To call it a lie is the understatement of the year. Of the three hundred or so girls that Xaviera or I know, maybe three have any money today. The usual girl, and it makes no difference what step up the ladder or hierarchy she is in, spends her money as fast as she makes it. The streetwalker usually has a pimp who takes it. The sophisticated girl who works for Xaviera spends it on expensive apartments, clothes, supporting young kids, has it stolen. The bar girls are lucky to make a few dollars

200

and have a roof over their heads. I would kill my daughter before I would allow her to hustle.

Q. *Have you ever made it with a man?*

In *Xaviera*, there is a chapter called "On Cupid's Shaft." I was the actual person involved. The guy was a friend of mine who kept after me for years. He was a good friend of the girl I went with for so long, named Irene. Xaviera had met him also and invited him to come to the apartment. I thought I'd even try it, but when he tried to kiss me, the ball game ended. I don't knock it for anyone else. Just for me. I tried it, and it didn't work out. *Period.*

Q. *How did Xaviera start writing for* Penthouse *magazine?*

I, as her manager, made the arrangements with Bob Guccione in London. Bob is a nice guy, as good as he is charming and handsome. Irv Billman is Bob's right-hand man and is a good-looking, smooth guy that has more girls chasing him than a telephone book has names. What girl could resist the three of us?

Vanessa Answers Questions

Q. *How did you feel when Larry, the Silver Fox, first asked you out?*

When Larry had asked me to have lunch with him, the first thought that crossed my mind was that I'd be seen with him and marked as a hooker. After all, this man *was* known as a pimp, and knew virtually every hooker in town. And doesn't a pimp get a percentage of his working girls?

"So what?" I rationalized. "If people I *know* see me with Larry, they *know* I'm not a hooker. And people who know Larry, but not me, might *think* I was a hooker."

Larry is no more a pimp than I am a hooker. He has never accepted money from a hooker or a hooker's client. He has suggested certain girls to contact, if and when certain guys asked him. And he did this more as a favor than anything else. No doubt, too, it boosted his ego to know that only *he* was asked to make a contact. Top company executives who look for hookers aren't man enough to admit that Larry did them a favor by calling ladies of the evening for them. It is much easier for them to put Larry down as a pimp and procurer who lives off hookers' fees, than to admit to themselves that they are in that sad group of males who have to pay for attention.

Q. *How is the Silver Fox in bed?*

Every punk in the West was ready to show Billy the Kid he was the fastest gun in the West by outdrawing Billy.

It's the same with every female who has followed the trail of the Silver Fox. Each one will show him *she's* the greatest lay—or else each one will be curious to discover what the Fox has to offer. Neither one of these things turned me on to the Silver Fox.

I wasn't one of those who tried to outdraw Billy the Kid, but I was one who had a love affair with the Silver Fox.

Neither one of us was out to prove anything to the other. We just pleased each other sexually because we wanted to—because there was a lot of emotion between us. He's not only great in bed, but anywhere we decide to make love. Remember, bed's not the only place . . .

Q. *Aren't you enraged when you think about a woman like Xaviera taking advantage of Larry's kindness?*

Regardless of her reputation, I admire the woman's honesty. Her writings have caused many people to come out of sexually-confining closets.

Do I resent her taking advantage of Larry? Yes, I do, only because I know Larry as a kind, generous, compassionate, fun-loving person who wants to be loved and has a lot of love to give. The formula is so simple, it's complicated. To be wanted, to belong, and to be needed are the three basic prerequisites between two people. If either one is looking for more than these simple basics, then they're searching for something that's non-existent.

Q. *How can you go with a guy who's been with a hooker for so long? You can't think much of yourself.*

Through confidence, and not vanity, I think a great deal of myself. I know who I am. Too many people seek to live their lives to please other people. One should be selfish enough to please oneself. When you have reached this plateau, only then can you please and accept others.

Larry's past I cannot mourn. Yesterday is gone

and tomorrow is beyond my reach, so what is important to me is "now"—it is the only reality.

Q. *Do you go for girls as well as guys?*

I don't put down homosexuality, but I do prefer men. I've never had sexual relations with a woman, but that doesn't mean I won't in the future. Right now I much prefer a man's chest against mine, instead of another pair of tits.

Q. *After reading Larry's first book* My Life With Xaviera, *I got the feeling he's trying to redeem himself. He sounds too nice. Is this a put-on? What's he really like is what I'm asking.*

Under that Silver Fox mantle, he's exactly what Xaviera described in her first book "a nice, straight, middle-aged man." He loves life, it's that simple.

Q. *Are there any secrets you don't dare tell?*

Several. But in this literary world certain things cannot be published that might be libelous or slanderous. I *can* tell you, however, that there are certain epistles I've read from Xaviera to Larry that could really rock her boat if Larry ever blows the whistle. He won't though. He's good that way.

Q. *Do you enjoy all forms of sex?*

Do birds fly?

Epilogue

To live for today and
Love for tomorrow
Is for but a fool
For tomorrow is not promised to anyone

I am so happy to see my second baby going to press. It's wonderful realizing that so many nice things have happened to me A.X. (after Xaviera). My feelings have always been that bigger and better things always lie ahead. Look to the future. And do exactly as you want ... as long as you don't hurt anyone while doing it.

My exciting adventures still afford me the opportunity to convey small messages to my readers about the things I still am learning every day of my life.

Oh, yeah! Congratulations are in order. Xaviera has married. We remain in constant contact with each other. She tells me it will last. God bless her. She deserves good luck . . .

I am still going with my gal (ninety-two weeks). Hope with my next book I can report another hundred weeks.

The serious novel I had been working on has ground to an abrupt halt. My indentity as the Silver Fox created an impasse. The manuscript is in a status quo condition. Maybe I'm too busy living it up to be able to get it down on paper.

And I've almost completed my third book on the do's & don'ts of sex. It's called *Hooker Happy*, and includes some hilarious and fascinating material about the world's most successful madams and hookers. It has been interesting research. In this book I also describe how anyone can become a "Silver Fox." This is hot stuff. I once said my life is just warming up, and I am not about to stop in my tracks.

So stay with me for my further adventures.

Larry, "The Silver Fox"

P.S. Y'know, certain things amuse me as I look back on them now, and I'd like to share them with you.

As Xaviera's manager, I had certain legal rights to all products that had anything whatsoever to do with Xaviera Hollander and/or "The Happy Hooker." Being her boyfriend *and* manager resulted in a relationship that was both emotional and businesslike. A helluva position.

It's funny though. When two people are in love, they promise each other *everything*—forever! That "forever" lasts until the love-bubble bursts! Then they become animals, clawing away at the things they once held dear.

The book you're holding now originally had a photo of Xaviera and me on the cover. This was legally sound, since I was part of the photo and had legal rights to do so. Right? Wrong! As soon as Xaviera and her attorney learned that the cover was to feature our photo, the fit hit the shan.

Reasons given included "her boyfriend (now husband) resented the idea of his wife's picture on the cover of a book with a former love," and "Xaviera's new book was to follow on the heels of publication of this book and would affect sales of her book," et cetera *ad nauseum*.

Now the real reason, I can tell you, is because I refused to give Xaviera a percentage of this book's sales, as I did with my previous book *My Life With Xaviera.*

But you can't blame her for wanting a piece. (No pun intended.) There are so, so many people making money from Xaviera's notoriety. Writers, attorneys, producers, so many. But that's the price Xaviera has to pay for her fame, from which came fortune.

Did Bruce Catton plan the Civil War so that he could later reap millions by writing about it? Exactly my sentiments.

And d'ya know something? I really don't care any more. I've risen above it. I'm my own free agent. I'm happy for my own existence, happy for the Happy Hooker, happy for being happy.

I'll just roll with the punches. And tomorrow ... well, tomorrow will take care of itself.

By the way, if you have not already done so, write to me about any of your problems or ideas, or to join the "Swingiest Group Around," the Silver Fox Fan Club. I personally answer every letter ever written to me. The address is:

> The Silver Fox
> P.O. Box 143
> Peck Slip Station
> New York City, NY 10038

of life no matter what calendar age you reach. It has long been known and accepted that the stars have an incredible influence on the kind of person you are—but what is little known is that they can help you to enjoy a healthy, youthful, sex-filled life right through your golden years.   **P016   95¢**

RECYCLE YOUR LIFESTYLE, by Dr. Paul Mok. This is a unique new system for reorganizing one's life and potentiating one's energy. Learn how to be that happier, more effective individual you really are! This book is deep in its meaning and its merit; however, it is written in easily understood language. The lessons are clear and the system is gradual. It is not an overnight overhaul of your life, but a reawakening and remodeling of your attitudes and ideas. It works!   **P118   95¢**

SCIENTIFIC ASTROLOGY, by Sir John Manolesco. Finally, the inside truth about astrology! Here is a clear, authoritative and absorbing look at a very old subject, one that has long been fascinating to both fans and cynics. It is a most unique exploration of an influential force at work on all of our lives. Sir John's book gives outsiders an inside look; the whole truth about astrology: the information necessary to evaluate any given astrological source.   **P176   95¢**

DREAM-SCOPE, by Sydney Omarr. Here, from the man named "Outstanding Contributor to the Advancement of Astrology," is a revolutionary method of tapping the world of dreams, of viewing them both in the form of written words and pictures. DREAM-SCOPE allows each reader to embark upon adventures previously confined to the world of sleep. All the mysteries of dream interpretation are revealed, permitting the reader to "see" his dream as he never could before—but always wanted to. From cover to cover, DREAM-SCOPE is a dream of a book.

P185   95¢

THE THIN BOOK BY A FORMERLY FAT PSYCHIATRIST, by Theodore Rubin, M.D. Dr. Rubin presents his very successful approach to weight control. With fewer words, easier dieting, no drugs, no magic, and absolutely no miracle exercise routines Dr. Rubin presents a no-nonsense handbook that will trim waistlines without starvation or acrobatics. His ideas are medically authoritative, scientifically accurate, and psychologically sound. This is the way to shave off from 5 to 50 or more pounds of excess blubber. It works!   **P077   95¢**

This is your Order Form . . .
Just clip and mail.

_____ P088 RELAXERCISES, Joan Fraser   1.25

_____ P098 EXECUTIVE YOGA, Harvey Day   1.25

_____ P135 MASSAGE: THE LOVING TOUCH, S. Lewis   1.95

_____ P016 STAY YOUNG WITH ASTROLOGY,
Frank McCarthy   .95

_____ P118 RECYCLE YOUR LIFESTYLE, Paul Mok   .95

_____ P176 SCIENTIFIC ASTROLOGY, John Manolesco   .95

_____ P185 DREAM-SCOPE, Sydney Omarr   .95

_____ P077 THE THIN BOOK BY A FORMERLY FAT
PSYCHIATRIST, Dr. Theodore Rubin   .95

TO ORDER

Please check the space next to the book/s you want, send this order form together with your check or money order, include the price of the book/s and 25¢ for handling and mailing, to:

PINNACLE BOOKS, INC. / P.O. Box 4347
Grand Central Station / New York, N. Y. 10017

☐ Check here if you want a free catalog.

I have enclosed $_____ check_____ or money order_____
as payment in full. No C.O.D.s.

Name_____

Address_____

City_____ State_____ Zip_____
(Please allow time for delivery.)

Sex, sociology & marriage books everyone is buying